GW00976564

Service of Documents

To Betty

Service of Documents

in High Court and County Court Proceedings

Second Edition

Anthony Radevsky LLB

Barrister
of the Inner Temple and South-Eastern Circuit

LONGMAN

© Longman Group UK Ltd 1989

ISBN 0 85121 609 9

First Edition 1982
Second Edition 1989

Published by
Longman Law, Tax and Finance
Longman Group UK Ltd
21–27 Lamb's Conduit Street
London WC1N 3NJ

Associated Offices
Australia, Hong Kong, Malaysia, Singapore, USA

A CIP catalogue record of this book is available
from the British Library

Printed and bound in Great Britain by
Biddles Ltd, Guildford and King's Lynn

Contents

Preface

In the seven years since the first edition of this book was published, there have been numerous procedural changes. The most important of these result from the coming into force on 1 January 1987 of the Civil Jurisdiction and Judgments Act 1982, together with new rules of court. This unduly complex new regime abolishes the requirement to obtain leave to serve process out of the jurisdiction in many cases. The advent of document exchanges and fax machines have also been noted in relation to service, and recent reported cases and amendments to the Rules of the Supreme Court, the County Court Rules and the Matrimonial Causes Rules are all incorporated into the text. It is hoped that this edition will prove to be a useful time saver. The law is stated as at 1 September 1989.

1 September 1989   *Anthony Radevsky*

Table of Cases

TABLE OF CASES   xi

Table of Statutes

Table of Rules

Abbreviations

CCR   County Court Rules 1981
MCA   Matrimonial Causes Act 1973
MCR   Matrimonial Causes Rules 1977
RSC   Rules of the Supreme Court 1965
RCJ   Royal Courts of Justice, Strand, London WC2

Reference to the *Supreme Court Practice* are to the 1988 edition (Sweet and Maxwell/Stevens and Sons 1988)

Part 1

Service within the Jurisdiction

The jurisdiction for the purposes of the service of documents comprises the whole of England and Wales, including the town of Berwick-upon-Tweed. Scotland, Northern Ireland, Eire, the Isle of Man and the Channel Islands are *not* within the jurisdiction.

Although it has not been conclusively decided whether the coastal limits of the jurisdiction are the low water mark or the limit of territorial waters, it is submitted that it is the latter (which is also the view of the editors of the *Supreme Court Practice*). By virtue of the Territorial Sea Act 1987, which came into force on 1 October 1987, the breadth of the territorial sea adjacent to the United Kingdom shall for all purposes be 12 nautical miles.

By a quaint, though still effective, legal fiction, a British man-of-war is deemed to be in the parish of Stepney and, therefore, always within the jurisdiction. Accordingly, service on an officer on board a ship of the Royal Navy should be effected without obtaining leave, even if it is anchored in Australia. Since, in those circumstances, it is inevitable that a longer than normal time will be required by the defendant to acknowledge service, the practice is to issue an ordinary writ and apply to the Practice Master on an affidavit in similar form to an application to serve out of the jurisdiction (see Chapter 16) for an extension of time (*Fraser* v *Akers* (1891) 35 SJ 477).

Chapter 1

High Court Writs

This chapter is concerned with the service of writs in the High Court, the procedure for which is governed primarily by RSC Ord 10, rr 1–4. However, these rules apply also, with any necessary modifications, to originating summonses, and r 1(1)–(4) applies, similarly, to notices of originating motion and to petitions. As to these other originating processes, see further Chapter 2. Particular procedures are prescribed in relation to service on specific defendants. As to these procedures, see Chapter 5.

1 Methods of service

Order 10, r 1(1),(2), as amended, reads as follows:

(1) A writ must be served personally on each defendant by the plaintiff or his agent.

(2) A writ for service on a defendant within the jurisdiction may, instead of being served personally on him, be served—

    (*a*) by sending a copy of the writ by ordinary first-class post to the defendant at his usual or last address, or

    (*b*) if there is a letter box for that address, by inserting through the letter box a copy of the writ enclosed in a sealed envelope addressed to the defendant.

In sub-paragraph *(a)* 'first-class post' means first-class post which has been pre-paid or in respect of which prepayment is not required.

The rules for personal and postal service are considered further under heads 5 and 6 below.

There are a number of exceptions to service under r 1(1) or (2), which were of more general importance before 1979 but which still apply:

(1) By Ord 10, r 1(4), where a defendant's solicitor indorses on the writ a statement that he accepts service of the writ on

behalf of that defendant, the writ shall be deemed to have been duly served on that defendant and to have been so served on the date on which the indorsement was made. The indorsement should be in the form:

I/We accept service hereof [*or* of the writ of summons/originating summons/etc] on behalf of the defendant, the . . . day of . . . 19 . . . . [*signature and address*].

Where the defendants' solicitors agreed to accept service, the defendant living abroad, service on them was held to be effective even though they later returned the writ marked 'service of writ accepted without prejudice to dispute jurisdiction'. (*Manta Line Inc* v *Seraphim Sofianites and Midland Bank plc* [1984] 1 Lloyd's Rep 15).

Solicitors should always be careful, however, to complete the acknowledgement of service stating the defendant's intention to defend the proceedings, since the indorsement alone is not sufficient.

(2) By Ord 10, r 1(5), subject to Ord 12, r 7 (for which see Chapter 8, head 1), where a writ is not duly served on a defendant but he acknowledges service of it, the writ shall be deemed, unless the contrary is shown, to have been duly served on him and to have been so served on the date on which he acknowledges service.

This paragraph is equivalent to the old practice of entering an appearance 'gratis'. A person may acknowledge service 'gratis' even after the validity of the writ has expired, ie, more than a year after issue (*The Gniezno* [1968] P 418). The date of service is deemed to be the date the Court Office receives the acknowledgement. The defendant should not acknowledge service 'gratis' after the plaintiff gives him notice that the writ is abandoned (*Oulton* v *Radcliffe* (1874) 9 LRCP 189). Further, a defendant who appears on a motion in the action may be treated as if service was good and acknowledged, even if there is no acknowledgement (*Boyer* v *Sacker* (1889) 39 Ch D 249). Where a person is made defendant to a counterclaim, and he is not already a party to the proceedings, he may acknowledge service of the counterclaim 'gratis' by virtue of this paragraph, see RSC Ord 15, r 3(5).

The words 'unless the contrary is shown' are to be given their ordinary meaning. Where plaintiffs issued a writ and sent a copy to the defendants' solicitors 'for information only', and those solicitors filed an acknowledgement of service and asked the plaintiffs for a statement of claim, the writ was held not to have been served at all (*Abu Dhabi Helicopters Ltd* v *International Aeradio plc* [1986] 1 WLR 312).

(3) By Ord 65, r 4, where an order for substituted service is made (see Chapter 7).

(4) By Ord 10, r 4, in an action for the possession of land, the court may authorise service of the writ to be effected by affixing a copy of the writ to some conspicuous part of the land (see further head 7 below).

(5) By Ord 77, r 4, a procedure is laid down for service on the Crown, for which see Chapter 5, head 1).

(6) By Ord 11, r 5(3), a procedure is detailed for service to be effected abroad in accordance with the local law, see Chapter 16.

(7) By Ord 75, rr 8, 11, procedures are laid down for the service of a writ in an Admiralty action in rem (see head 9 below).

(8) By Ord 113, r 4, procedures are laid down for the service of an originating summons in squatters' proceedings (see Chapter 2, head 1).

2 Who may be served

Subject to the exception of privileged persons, any defendant, British or foreign, may be served with a writ. The exception relates to ambassadors or ministers of foreign states in England and Wales, and to members of foreign embassies, and in those cases the writ is null and void. For authorities on the extent of this diplomatic immunity, see the *Supreme Court Practice*, para 65/2/3.

3 Where service may be effected

Prima facie, service may be effected anywhere within the jurisdiction. However, the four places indicated below require further consideration:

(1) It is frequently tempting to consider serving a document on a person within the precincts of a court. Nevertheless, because of the possibility that such service might amount to a contempt of court, it should be avoided if possible. In *R* v *Jones, ex parte McVittie* [1931] 1 KB 664 Lord Hewart CJ

said at p 670: 'I do not say that there may not be circumstances in which the service of process within the precincts of a Court may amount to contempt.' However, MacKinnon J, agreeing, added at p 671: 'Personally I cannot conceive what those circumstances could be.' In *Pook* v *Gould* (1856) 1 H & N 99 the defendant was served in a court where he was a witness in another case, and the court refused to set aside service of the writ. That decision was followed by the Divisional Court in *R* v *Barnet County Court, ex parte Brantschen* (1970) 115 SJ 60, which held that service of county court proceedings within the precincts of the High Court of Justice was valid. In the light of *McVittie's* case, the court repeated that, whilst service was valid, it might constitute contempt.

(2) According to the *Supreme Court Practice*, para 65/2/5, service of a writ within the precincts of a royal palace which is a residence of the Sovereign would probably be held invalid, even if the Monarch was absent at the time. Accordingly this practice should be avoided.

(3) The Committee of Privileges of the House of Commons has rules that it is a breach of privilege to serve a summons within the precincts of Parliament on a day when the House is sitting, even if the House is not in session at the moment of service.

(4) Where the defendant is in prison, the plaintiff should apply to the governor of that prison, and he will afford facilities for service. Where a governor refused admission, a rule nisi for attachment was granted (*Danson* v *Le Capelain* (1852) 21 LJ Ex 219). If it is not known in which prison the defendant is incarcerated, this information is obtainable from HM Prison Service Headquarters, Cleland House, Page Street, London SW1P 4LN, who will assist if details of the defendant's conviction etc can be provided.

4 Time for service

A writ, provided that it is valid (see Ord 6, r 8), may be served at any time of the day or night on any day of the week, except Sundays (Ord 65, r 10). However, r 10(1) provides that process may be served or executed within the jurisdiction on a Sunday, with the leave of the court, in case of urgency. This exception will be useful where, for instance, the defendant is about to leave the jurisdiction in a hurry; but the plaintiff will have to show that it is a real emergency before the court will grant leave. Clearly, if at all possible, leave should be obtained in advance; but if service takes place on a Sunday without prior leave, it may be possible to correct the irregularity using Ord 2, by subsequent leave being granted by the court.

It should be noted that service outside the jurisdiction is not affected by this rule. Note also that Ord 75, r 11(3), provides that Ord 65, r 10, does not apply in relation to a warrant of arrest or writ in rem (and see head 9 below).

5 Personal service

Ord 65, r 2, as amended, deals with the service of *all* documents in the High Court. It provides that personal service of a document is effected by leaving a copy of the document with the person to be served. The former requirement that the writ had to be shown to the defendant on request has been abolished. The process server should make sure that he has correctly identified the defendant, and then either hand the document to him or leave it with him. If the defendant refuses to take it, the server should tell him what it contains and leave it as nearly in his possession or control as possible in the circumstances.

There are numerous, mostly nineteenth century, authorities on what amounts to good or bad personal service. The following are some reported examples of *bad* service:

(1) A copy of the writ was pushed through a crevice of the door of a room in which the defendant was and the latter was told what the document was (*Christmas* v *Eicke* (1848) 6 D&L 156).

(2) A process server outside the defendant's house called out to the defendant, who was at an upper window, that he had a writ against him and held up a copy for the defendant to see. He then threw the copy down in the presence of the defendant's wife (*Heath* v *White* (1844) 2 D&L 40).

(3) A process server placed the copy into a basket which had been put over the garden wall by the defendant's servant. Immediately afterwards the server heard the defendant saying to the servant 'take it back, I won't have it', and the servant at a later date told the server that she had given the copy to the defendant (*Goggs* v *Lord Huntingtower* (1844) 12 M&W 503).

(4) The defendant was handed the copy writ in a closed

envelope without being told the contents (*Banque Russe* v *Clarke* [1894] WN 203).

(5) The wife/known agent of the defendant was served (*Frith* v *Lord Donegal* (1834) 2 DPC 527), sed contra where the defendant requests service on his wife/agent (*Montgomery & Co* v *Liebenthal & Co* [1898] 1 QB 487).

(6) The server brought the copy away from the defendant, having shown him it (*Pigeon* v *Bruce* (1818) 8 Taunt 410).

However, if the defendant refuses to accept the copy, it is sufficient to inform him of its nature and throw it onto the floor in his presence (*Thomson* v *Pheney* (1832) 1 DPC 441).

The extent to which the server may touch the person to be served was discussed in the interesting case of *Rose* v *Kempthorne* (1910) 103 LT 730. Here, the Divisional Court allowed an appeal against conviction by justices for assault by a person who had attempted to serve personally the plaintiff in a civil action. After the plaintiff refused to accept service, the appellant 'thrust the document into the inner fold of the respondent's coat, which was unbuttoned at the time, and the respondent opened his coat, causing the document to fall into the gutter . . .'. Lord Alverstone CJ said at p 731: 'In this case, as the appellant had before him the respondent, whom he was entitled to serve personally, and who would not receive the document, I think that touching the respondent was not unnecessary under the circumstances. All the appellant did was to endeavour to place the document in the fold of the respondent's coat, and there was really no evidence that the appellant touched the respondent further than was necessary to bring the document home to him.'

Provided that any error or omission in the copy of the writ served is minor and immaterial, it will not vitiate the service (*Hanmer* v *Clifton* [1894] 1 QB 238). Though the omission of the Division of the High Court to which the action was assigned, or the name of the District Registry out of which the writ was issued, is material, the irregularity may be corrected under Ord 2, and the proceedings are not thereby automatically nullified (*Brady* v *Barrow Steel Works Ltd* [1965] 2 QB 182).

6 Postal service

Ord 10, r 1(2), set out in head 1 above, is largely self-explanatory, though a few points must be noted.

In a recent case the House of Lords has held that, for the

purposes of Ord 10, r 1(2), the defendant had to be within the jurisdiction at the time of service of the writ (*Barclays Bank of Swaziland Ltd v Hahn* [1989] 1 WLR 506). The plaintiff had inserted the writ through the defendant's letter box at a time when he believed him to be there. The defendant was in fact flying to England at that moment and, being warned that the envelope had been put through the letter box, flew straight back without visiting his flat. Service was held to be good since the plaintiff could show for the purposes of r 1(3)(a) that the deemed service of the writ was not seven days after its insertion through the letter box, but the day of insertion, when there was no doubt that the copy writ came to the knowledge of the defendant when he was within the jurisdiction.

Rule 1(2)(a) specifies ordinary first-class post and the plaintiff must not attempt to go one better and use registered post or recorded delivery, which would be available for the service of other documents under RSC Ord 65, r 5. It would seem that the reasoning behind this is to allow the defendant to refuse to accept the letter, in the same way that he could attempt to avoid personal service.

The words 'last known address' mean last known to the plaintiff (*Austin Rover Group Ltd v Crouch Butler Savage Associates* [1986] 1 WLR 1102, per May LJ at p 1111.)

Rule 1(3), provides that where a writ is served in accordance with r 1(2), the date of service will, unless the contrary is shown, be deemed to be the seventh day (ignoring Ord 3, r 2(5)) after the date on which the copy was sent to or, as the case may be, inserted through the letter box for the address in question. Order 3, r 2(5), excludes, in the reckoning of periods of time up to seven days, Saturdays, Sundays, bank holidays, Christmas Day and Good Friday. Since this subrule is to be ignored, those days are *included* in the calculation.

Sending a copy of the writ means not merely putting it in the post but the whole process of transmission from server to recipient. Actual receipt by the defendant amounted to good service even though the writ had been incorrectly addressed when posted (*Austin Rover* case).

The seven day period starts to run on the day after the letter was posted or inserted through the letter-box. If the seventh day falls on a day when the court offices are closed, the period will have expired by the next day on which they are open.

The words 'unless the contrary is shown' leave it open to the defendant to show that either he did not receive the copy writ at all, or that he received it later than the seven day period provided. Equally, the plaintiff may rely on those words to establish that the writ was served less than seven days after posting (*Hodgson* v *Hart District Council* [1986] 1 WLR 317). It should be noted that where a company is served under s 725 of the Companies Act 1985 (see Chapter 5, head 5), the seven day rule does not apply and the date of service will depend on whether first or second class mail is used (see Chapter 3, head 2).

It should be noted that r 1(3)(*a*) is consistent with the cases which have held that:

(1) proof that a letter has been properly addressed, prepaid and posted to the proper address of the person to be served and *not* returned through the Post Office undelivered to the addressee, is prima facie evidence of due delivery to the addressee (*A/S Catherineholm* v *Norequipment Trading Ltd* [1972] 2 QB 314); and

(2) where the letter is so returned undelivered, through the Post Office, it will be regarded as not having been served (*R* v *London County Quarter Sessions Appeal Committee, ex parte Rossi* [1956] 1 QB 682).

These words make it plain that the 'letter-box' connotes the colloquial term of a slit or hole in the outside door of the premises, which may or may not have a box behind it to catch the letters. It will include a letter-box placed at the side of the front door or, American-style, at the street end of a front garden path. On the other hand, the words seemingly do not include personal delivery to a caretaker or other person on the premises, who may have opened the door to the process server.

Though the editors of the *Supreme Court Practice* take the view that pushing the envelope under the door or through an open door are excluded, it is the author's view that these methods may in certain circumstances be acceptable if, for instance, there is no conventional letter-box in the front door, or the door has been left wide open.

7 Actions for possession of land

By Ord 10, r 4(*a*), where a writ is indorsed with a claim for the possession of land, the Court may, if satisfied on an ex parte application that no person appears to be in possession of the land and that service cannot be otherwise effected on any defendant, authorise service on that defendant to be effected by affixing a copy of the writ to some conspicuous part of the land.

The application is made by affidavit to a master, which is left at the Masters' Secretary's Department, RCJ, and collected later with the master's decision indorsed on it. The affidavit must show what efforts have been made to serve the writ ordinarily and why service cannot be effected. If the defendant is thought to be abroad, this must be deposed to. Once service is effected under this rule, judgment in default of acknowledgement of service can only be entered for possession of the land. Judgment for arrears of rent etc may only be entered after an order for substituted service under Ord 65, r 4, has been made, though both applications can be made in the same affidavit.

Where service in this manner has been effected before the application is made, the court may order that such service be treated as good service, provided the application is made as above (Ord 10, r 4(*b*)). If fourteen days have elapsed since such service, the plaintiff may enter judgment in default of acknowledgement of service.

8 Service pursuant to contract

By Ord 10, r 3(1), where:

   (*a*) a contract contains a term to the effect that the High Court shall have jurisdiction to hear and determine any action in respect of a contract or, apart from any such term, the High Court has jurisdiction to hear and determine any such action (eg under Ord 11, r 1); and

   (*b*) the contract provides that, in the event of any action in respect of the contract being begun, the process by which it is begun may be served on the defendant, or on such other person on his behalf as may be specified in the contract, in such manner, or at such place (whether within or out of the jurisdiction), as may be so specified,

then if a writ by which an action in respect of the contract is begun is served in accordance with the contract, it will be deemed to have been duly served on the defendant. However, a writ which is served out of the jurisdiction in accordance with a contract is not deemed to be due service unless leave to serve the writ out of the jurisdiction has been granted under Ord 11, r 1 (Ord 10, r 3(2)). This is subject to r 3(3), which provides that where a contract contains an agreement conferring jurisdiction to which Article 17 of Sched 1 or of Sched 4 to the Civil Jurisdiction and Judgments Act 1982 applies, and the writ is served under Ord 11, r 1(2), the writ is deemed to be duly served on the defendant (see also Chapter 14).

9 Admiralty proceedings

By Ord 75, r 8(1), subject to r 8(2), a writ by which an action in rem is begun must be served on the property against which the action is brought except:

(a) where the property is freight, in which case it must be served on the cargo in respect of which the freight is payable or on the ship in which that cargo was carried; or

(b) where that property has been sold by the marshal, the writ may not be served on that property but a sealed copy of it must be filed in the registry or, if the writ was issued out of a district registry, in that registry, and the writ shall be deemed to have been duly served on the day on which the copy was filed.

Rule 8(2) provides that the exceptions in Ord 10, r 1(4), (5) (see head 1 above) apply here.

Rule 8(3) provides that where by virtue of r 8 a writ is required to be served on any property, the plaintiff may request service to be effected by the marshal if, but only if, a warrant of arrest has been issued for service against the property or the property is under arrest, and in that case the plaintiff must file in the registry or, in an action proceeding in a district registry, that registry a praecipe in Form 6 in Appendix B and lodge the writ and a copy thereof, and an undertaking to pay on demand all expenses issued by the marshal or his substitute in respect of the service of the writ. Thereupon the marshal or his substitute must serve the writ on the property described in the praecipe.

Where the writ is so served, the marshal or his substitute must indorse on the writ the following information (r 8(3A)):

(a) where it was served;

(b) the property on which it was served;

(c) the day of the week and date of service;

(d) the manner in which it was served; and

(e) the name and address of the server.

The indorsement is then evidence of the facts stated therein (ibid).

Where the plaintiff in an action in rem, or his solicitor, becomes aware that there is in force a caveat against arrest (under Ord 75, r 6) with respect to the property against which the action is brought, he must serve the writ forthwith on the person at whose instance the caveat was entered (Ord 75, r 8(4)).

Where a writ by which an action in rem is begun is amended under Ord 20, r 1, after service, Ord 20, r 1(2) (see head 10 below), does not apply and, unless the court otherwise directs on an application made ex parte, the amended writ must be served on any intervener and any defendant who has acknowledged issue or service of the writ in the action or, if no defendant has acknowledged issue or service of the writ, it must be served or filed in accordance with r 8(1) (above) (r 8(5)).

A warrant of arrest issued under Ord 75, r 5, may be executed (ie served) only by the marshal or his substitute, and is valid for twelve months after being issued (r 10(1), (2)). It is served in accordance with Ord 75, r 11 (see below).

A warrant of arrest will not be executed until an undertaking to pay on demand the fees of the marshal and all expenses incurred by him or on his behalf in respect of the arrest of the property and the care and custody of it while under arrest has been lodged in the marshal's office or, where the action is proceeding in a district registry, in that registry (r 10(3)). Nor will it be executed if the party at whose instance it was issued lodges a written request to that effect with the marshal or, where the action is proceeding in a district registry, the registrar of that registry (r 10(4)).

A warrant of arrest issued against freight may be executed by serving the warrant on the cargo in respect of which the freight is payable or on the ship in which that cargo was carried or on both of them (r 10(5)). Any other warrant must be served on the property against which it was issued.

By r 10(7), within seven days after the service of a warrant of arrest, the warrant must be filed (*a*) where it was issued out of the registry, in the registry by the marshal, and (*b*) where it was issued out of a district registry, in that registry by the party who procured it to be issued (eg, the plaintiff's solicitor).

By r 11(1), subject to r 11(2), service of a warrant of arrest or writ in an action in rem against a ship, freight or cargo must be effected by:

(*a*) affixing it for a short time on any mast of the ship or on the outside of any suitable part of the ship's superstructure; and

(*b*) on removing it, leaving a copy of it affixed (in the case of the warrant) in its place or (in the case of the writ) on a sheltered conspicuous part of the ship.

Rule 11(2) provides that service of a warrant of arrest or writ in an action in rem against freight or cargo or both must, if the cargo has been landed or trans-shipped, be effected:

(a) by placing it for a short time on the cargo, and on removing it, leaving a copy of it on the cargo; or

(b) if the cargo is in the custody of a person who will not permit access to it, by leaving a copy of it with that person.

Service may be effected on a Sunday (r 11(3) and Ord 65, r 10).

A notice of motion (except a motion for judgment in default) must be served on all caveators, together with copies of any affidavits in support, at least two clear days before the hearing, unless the court gives leave to the contrary (Ord 75, r 34(2)). Unless the court gives leave to the contrary, the affidavits must be filed in the appropriate registry before the notice of motion is issued (r 34(1)).

The writ in a limitation action must be served on one or more of the defendants who are named by their names therein, and need not be served on any other defendant (Ord 75, r 37(4)).

Where a summons for a decree or directions is taken out under Ord 75, r 38, it, together with any affidavit in support, must be served at least seven clear days before the hearing of the summons on any defendant who has acknowledged issue or service of the writ.

10 Amended writs

By RSC Ord 20, r 1(1), subject to r 1(3), the plaintiff may, without the leave of the court, amend the writ once at any time before the pleadings in the action begun by the writ are deemed to be closed.

Where a writ is amended under r 1(1) after the original writ has been served, then, unless the court directs otherwise on an ex parte application, the amended writ must be served on each defendant to the action (r 1(2)). Where the amendment is made before service is acknowledged, service must be in accordance with RSC Ord 10. Where the amendment is made after acknowledgement of service, the court may dispense with service of the amended writ or order ordinary service under RSC Ord 65, r 5. The original acknowledgement of service stands good to the amended writ. Where the amendment is made before the original writ was served, service must be under Ord 10 as if it were the original writ.

Rule 1(3) provides that r 1 does not apply in relation to an amendment which consists of:

(*a*) the addition, omission or substitution of a party to the action or an alteration of the capacity in which a party to the action sues or is sued; or

(*b*) the addition or substitution of a new cause of action; or

(*c*) (without prejudice to r 3(1)) an amendment of the statement of claim (if any) indorsed on the writ on any party to the action.

Order 20, r 3(1) provides that a party may, without leave, amend any pleading of his once at any time before the pleadings are deemed to be closed and, where he does so, he must serve the amended pleading on the opposite party.

Where a defendant is added or substituted as a party to an action under Ord 15, r 6, he must be served with the amended writ as if it were the original writ (Ord 15, r 8(2)). The rules as to acknowledgement of service apply to such a defendant (r 8(3)).

Chapter 2

Other High Court Originating Process

Rules 1–4 of RSC Ord 10 (dealing with service of writs: see Chapter 1) apply, with any necessary modifications, in relation to an originating summons (other than an ex parte originating summons or an originating summons under Ord 113) as they apply in relation to a writ, except that an acknowledgement of service of an originating summons is in Form 15 in Appendix A (Ord 10, r 5(1)). Further, r 1(1)–(4) applies, with any necessary modifications, in relation to a notice of an originating motion and a petition, as it applies in relation to a writ (Ord 10, r 5(2)). In addition the following rules apply to service of other originating process.

1 Originating summonses for possession of land

Order 113, r 4(1) provides that, where any person in occupation of the land is named in the originating summons for the possession of the land, the summons together with a copy of the affidavit in support must be served on him:

  (a) personally; or
  (b) by leaving a copy of the summons and of the affidavit or sending them to him, at the premises; or
  (c) in such other manner as the court may direct.

The summons must, by r 4(2), in addition to being served on the named defendants, if any, in accordance with r 4(1) be served on unnamed defendants, unless the court otherwise directs, by:

  (a) affixing a copy of the summons and a copy of the affidavit to the main door or other conspicuous part of the premises and, if practicable, inserting through the letter-box at the premises a copy of the summons and a copy of the affidavit enclosed in a sealed transparent envelope addressed to 'the occupiers', or

(b) placing stakes in the ground at conspicuous parts of the occupied land, to each of which shall be affixed a sealed transparent envelope addressed to 'the occupiers' and containing a copy of the summons and affidavit.

Every copy of an originating summons for service under r 4(1) or (2) must be sealed with the seal of the office of the Supreme Court out of which the summons was issued (r 4(2A)).

In *Greater London Council* v *Tully* (1976) 120 SJ 555, a summons under Ord 113 was issued against certain named defendants and against persons unknown. It was held that, though service in accordance with r 4(2) was valid against the unknown occupiers, it was not valid against the named defendants, each of whom had to be served separately under r 4(1).

Order 28, r 3, which requires four clear days notice to be given of the hearing in an ordinary originating summons action, does not apply to proceedings under Ord 113 (r 4(3)).

2 Petitions

Ord 9, r 4(2), provides that unless the court otherwise directs, a petition which is required to be served on any person must be served on him not less than seven days before the day fixed for the hearing of the petition.

Winding-up petitions

Service of a winding-up petition (where the petitioner is other than the company itself) is governed by r 4.8 of the Insolvency Rules 1986. The petition must be served at the company's registered office, that is to say:

(a) the place specified in the company's statement delivered under s 10 of the Companies Act 1985 as the intended situation of its registered office on incorporation; or

(b) if notice has been given by the company to the registrar of companies under s 287 of the 1985 Act (change of registered office), the place specified in that notice or, as the case may be, in the last such notice.

By r 4.8(3), the following alternative methods of service are prescribed:

(a) it may be handed to a person who there and then

acknowledges himself to be, or to the best of the server's knowledge, information and belief is, a director or other officer, or employee of the company; or

(b) it may be handed to a person who there and then acknowledges himself to be authorised to accept service of documents on the company's behalf; or

(c) in the absence of any such person as is mentioned in (a) or (b) it may be deposited at or about the registered office in such a way that it is likely to come to the notice of a person attending at the office.

If for any reason service at the registered office is not practicable, or the company has no registered office, or it is an unregistered company, the petition may be served at the company's last known principal place of business in England and Wales, or at some place in England and Wales at which it has carried on business, by handing it to such a person as is mentioned in (a) or (b) above.

In the case of an overseas company, service may be effected under s 695 of the Companies Act 1985, for which see Chapter 5, head 5.

If it is impracticable to effect service as provided, the petition may be served in such other manner as the court may direct; the application for leave being made ex parte on affidavit stating what steps have been taken to comply with the rules and the reasons why such service is impracticable (r 4.8(6) and (7)).

Bankruptcy petitions

By r 6.14 of the Insolvency Rules 1986, a bankruptcy petition must in the first instance be served personally on the debtor by delivering to him a sealed copy of the petition. The server must be an officer of the court, the petitioning creditor or his solicitor, or a person instructed by the petitioning creditor or his solicitor (for personal service see Chapter 1, head 5).

If the court is satisfied by affidavit or other evidence on oath that prompt personal service cannot be effected because the debtor is keeping out of the way to avoid service of the petition or other legal process, or for any other cause, it may order substituted service to be effected in such manner as it thinks fit, which will then be deemed good service (r 6.14(2) and (3)). Details of what the court requires to be shown before it will order substituted service are set out in *Practice Note (Bankruptcy: Substituted Service)* [1987] 1 WLR 82, and see Chapter 7.

If the debtor dies before service of the petition, the court may order service to be effected on his personal representatives, or on such other persons as it thinks fit (r 6.16).

3 Garnishee proceedings

Where an application for a garnishee order under RSC Ord 49 is made and it is hoped to attach the defendant's bank account, the order must be served at the registered office (ie, normally the Head Office) of the bank, though the supporting affidavit must state the name and address of the branch where the account is held.

By Ord 49, r 3(1), unless the court otherwise directs, an order under Ord 49, r 1 to show cause must be served:

(*a*) on the garnishee personally, at least 15 days before the day appointed thereby for the further consideration of the matter; and

(*b*) on the judgment debtor, at least seven days after the order has been served on the garnishee and at least seven days before the day appointed for the further consideration of the matter.

Substituted service on the garnishee may be ordered in an appropriate case (see Chapter 7). Service on the judgment debtor may be by any method set out in Ord 65, r 5 (see Chapter 3). Service may be dispensed with if the debtor has had notice by letter of the application to make the order absolute and a reasonable opportunity to attend himself or by a solicitor. It should be noted that, since the amendment of this rule in 1981, the judgment debtor must be served after the garnishee, and para 49/3/1 of the 1988 Supreme Court Practice is incorrect in suggesting otherwise.

By r 3(2), an order under r 1 binds in the hands of the garnishee as from the service of the order on him any debt specified in the order or so much of it as may be so specified.

4 Interpleader proceedings

An application for interpleader relief is made either by originating summons or, if in a pending action, by action, by summons (Ord 17, r 3(1)), and the normal modes of service apply. Where the applicant is a sheriff who has taken goods in execution, a person making a claim in respect of the goods must give notice of his claim to the sheriff, and include his address (which is then his address for service). The sheriff then gives notice to the execution creditor who in turn must, within seven days after receipt of the notice, give notice to the sheriff saying whether or not he disputes the claim. If the claim is disputed, the matter is referred to court (Ord 17, r 2). Where the summons is taken out by the sheriff, it must be served on any person who made a claim under r 2(4).

Otherwise, where the summons is taken out under r 1(*a*) by a person under liability in respect of a debt, goods etc who expects two or more claims, it must be served on each claimant.

5 Mortgage actions

In a mortgage action under Ord 88 the proceedings should, if possible, be served on all the defendants. Where it is not possible to serve them all the court will proceed to make an order against the others where the persons not served would not be prejudiced (*Alliance Building Society* v *Shave* [1952] Ch 581).

Where the mortgagor cannot be served and substituted service is not ordered, the occupiers will have to be made defendants, which may be impracticable. If the mortgagor is managing the property himself or through an agent, an order for substituted service should be obtained. The summons may then be affixed to the premises.

Where a mortgagee claims possession etc, and a defendant fails to acknowledge service of the originating summons, Ord 88, r 4, provides the procedure to be followed.

By r 4(2), not less than four clear days before the day fixed for the first hearing of the originating summons, the plaintiff must serve on the defendant a copy of the notice of appointment of the hearing and a copy of the affidavit in support of the summons. By Ord 3, r 2(5) Saturdays, Sundays etc are not included.

By r 4(3), where the plaintiff claims possession, there must be indorsed on the outside fold of the copy affidavit served on the defendant a notice informing him that the plaintiff intends at the hearing to apply for an order that the defendant deliver up possession of the mortgaged property to the plaintiff and for any other relief that may be claimed under the originating summons at the hearing.

Where the hearing is adjourned, then, subject to any directions given by the court, the plaintiff must serve notice of the appointment for the adjourned hearing, together with a copy of any further affidavit intended to be used at that hearing (indorsed as above), on the defendant not less than two clear days before the hearing date (r 4(4)).

Service under r 4(2) or (4), and the manner in which it was effected, may be proved by a certificate signed by the plaintiff, if he sues in person, and otherwise by his solicitor. The certificate may be indorsed on the affidavit in support of the summons or, as the case may be, on any further affidavit intended to be used at an adjourned hearing (r 4(5)). Copies of any exhibits need not be served with an affidavit served under r 4(2) or (4) (r 4(6)).

There are no prescribed forms for notices under r 4(3) or (4) or a certificate under r 5(5), but forms which may be used are set out in the *Supreme Court Practice*, para 88/2–7/11. Where the plaintiff gives notice to the defendant under RSC Ord 3, r 6, of his intention to proceed, service of the notice, and the manner in which it was effected, may be proved by a certificate signed as in r 5(5)(r 5(7)).

6 Notices of motion

Unless the court gives leave to the contrary, there must be at least two clear days between the service of a notice of motion and the day named in it for the hearing (Ord 8, r 2(2)). Notice of a motion to be made in an action may be served on the defendant with the writ or originating summons or at any time after such service, whether or not the defendant has acknowledged service (r 4). An acknowledgement of service to a notice of originating motion is not required, although a respondent must acknowledge service before he may be heard in the action.

Leave to serve short notice of motion may be applied for by an ex parte application to a judge (not a master) in appropriate circumstances. In the Queen's Bench Division the application is made in chambers. In the Chancery Division the application is generally made after the midday adjournment.

Service of a notice of motion to quash or prohibit an order, scheme, certificate or plan of a minister under RSC Ord 94, r 1, is governed by Ord 94, r 2. It must be served within the time limited by the relevant Act for making the application by motion (r 2(1)). The notice is entered at the Crown Office.

Rule 2(2) provides that, subject to r 2(4), the notice of motion must be served on the appropriate minister or government department, and:

(*a*) if the application relates to a compulsory purchase order made by an authority other than the appropriate minister or government department (see below), or to a clearance order under the Housing Act 1957 [now see Housing Act 1985], on the authority by whom the order was made;

(*b*) if the application relates to a scheme or order to which the Highways Act 1980, Sched 2, applies, made by an authority other than the Secretary of State, on that authority;

(*c*) if the application relates to a structure plan, local or other development plan within the meaning of the Town and Country Planning Act 1971, on the local planning authority who prepared the plan;

(*d*) if the application relates to any decision or order, or any action on the part of a minister of the Crown to which the Land Compensation Act 1961, s 21, or the Town and Country Planning Act 1971, s 245 applies, on the authority directly concerned with that decision, order or action or, if that authority is the applicant, on every person who would, if he were aggrieved by the decision, order or action, be entitled to apply to the High Court under those sections.

Rule 2(3) defines 'the appropriate minister or government department' in r 2(2)(*a*) as the minister of the Crown or government department by whom the order, scheme, certificate, plan, amendment, approval or decision in question was made, authorised, confirmed, approved or given or on whose part the action in question was taken.

By r 2(4) in applications relating to orders made under the Road Traffic Regulation Act 1984, the notice of the motion must be served:

(*a* if the order was made by a minister of the Crown, on that minister;

(*b*) if the order was made by a local authority with the consent, or in pursuance of a direction, of a minister of the Crown, on that authority and also on that minister;

(*c*) in any other case, on the local authority by whom the order was made. 'Local authority' includes the Greater London Council.

The affidavit in support of the application if filed in the Crown Office within fourteen days after service of the notice of motion and a copy of it and exhibits must be served on the respondent at the time of filing.

For service on ministers, see Chapter 5. As to appeals to the

High Court by notice of motion under various specific statutes, see Ord 94, rr 6–15.

If a notice of an interlocutory motion is not served with the writ or originating summons under Ord 8, and is not a notice of motion to commit (see Chapter 3, head 7), it is served under Ord 65, r 5.

Chapter 3

Other High Court Documents

Any document required to be served on a person under the RSC need only be served personally where an express rule or court order so requires (RSC Ord 65, r 1). In the absence of such a rule or order requiring personal service and except in the case of a document to which RSC Ord 10, r 1, applies (eg a writ or originating summons), RSC Ord 65, r 5, provides the method of service, called 'ordinary service'.

However, r 5(3) provides that 'Nothing in this rule shall be taken as prohibiting the personal service of any document or as affecting any enactment which provides for the manner in which documents may be served on bodies corporate.' As to personal service, see Chapter 1.

Rule 5(1) provides four alternative ways of effecting ordinary service: by leaving the document at the proper address, by post, through a document exchange, or in such manner as the court may direct. The first three methods are dealt with in turn below. Service of certain specific documents is considered thereafter. As to service on certain specific defendants, see Chapter 5.

As a general principle, if the document to be served is shown to have been received, eg, if the recipient appears on the hearing of a summons, service will be good. Otherwise, proof of one of the prescribed methods will have to be shown. Service of a pleading by fax (facsimile transmission) was said obiter by the Court of Appeal to be good service, provided a legible copy of the document could be shown to have been received: *Ralux NV/SA* v *Spencer, The Times*, 18 May 1989. Equally, if in fact the document is shown not to have been received, eg if it is returned through the post unopened, good service will not be established.

Note that where by virtue of the rules any document is required to be served on any person but is not required to be served personally or in accordance with Ord 10, r 1(2), and at the time when service is to be effected that person is in default as to acknowledgement of service or has no address for service, the document need not be served on that person unless the court otherwise directs or any rule otherwise provides (Ord 65, r 9).

1 Leaving the document at the proper address

A person may be served with a document by leaving it at the proper address of the person to be served (Ord 65, r 5(1)(*a*)).

The 'proper address' for service of the person to be served is defined by Ord 65, r 5(2) and the Interpretation Act 1978, s 7, as the address for service of that person. The 'address for service' in turn depends on the status of the party to be served, ie plaintiff or defendant.

Order 65, r 5(2), provides that the address for service of a plaintiff is:

(*a*) where he sues by a solicitor, the business address (to which may be added a numbered box at a document exchange) of the solicitor indorsed on the writ or where there are two such addresses indorsed, the business address of the solicitor who is acting as agent for the other;

(*b*) where he sues in person, the address within the jurisdiction indorsed on the writ.

By virtue of Ord 12, r 3(2), the address for service of a defendant is specified in the acknowledgement of service and is:

(*a*) in the case of a defendant acknowledging service in person, the address of his place of residence and, if his place of residence is not within the jurisdiction or if he has no place of residence, the address of a place within the jurisdiction at or to which documents for him may be delivered or sent; and

(*b*) in the case of a defendant acknowledging service by a solicitor, a business address (to which may be added a numbered box at a document exchange) of his solicitor's within the jurisdiction.

Where the defendant acknowledges service in person, the address within the jurisdiction specified in (*a*) will be his address for service, but otherwise his solicitor's business address will be his address for service (ibid). In relation to a body corporate the references to the defendant's place of residence are to be construed as references to the defendant's registered or principal office (ibid).

Where one solicitor acts as agent for another for a defendant, he must also state that fact and give the name and address of the other solicitor (r 3(3)).

Further, by r 3(4), if an acknowledgement of service does not specify the defendant's address for service or the court is satisfied that any address specified in the acknowledgement of service is not genuine, the court may, on application by the plaintiff, set aside the acknowledgement or order the defendant to give an address or, as the case may be, a genuine address for service. The court may in any case direct that the acknowledgement shall neverthe-less have effect for the purposes of RSC Ord 10, r 1(5) (see Chapter 1, head 1) and Ord 65, r 9 (see above).

Where the defendant is in prison, he may give his address for service as the prison c/o the Home Office.

A party or his solicitor who changes his address for service must as soon as practicable after it occurs give notice in writing of such change of address to every other party, and to the Action Department who must, provided that the address is correct, record the new address in the Cause book.

By Ord 67, r 7, where a solicitor acting for a party is removed or withdraws, or the party's legal aid certificate is revoked or discharged, unless and until the party appoints another solicitor and gives notice or gives notice of intention to act in person, his address for service is deemed to be his last known address or, in the case of a body corporate, its registered or principal office.

If at the time when service is effected the person to be served has no address for service, Ord 65, r 5(2), provides that his proper address for such purposes is:

(*a*) in any case, the business address of the solicitor (if any) who is acting for him in the proceedings in connection with which service of the document in question is to be effected;

(*b*) in the case of an individual, his usual or last known address;

(*c*) in the case of individuals who are suing or being sued in the name of a firm, the principal or last known place of business of the firm within the jurisdiction; or

(*d*) in the case of a body corporate, the registered or principal office of the body.

'Leaving' the document at the proper address includes pushing it through the letter-box and leaving it with someone resident at the address, though in the case of a block of flats or an office block, it would not be sufficient to leave it with a caretaker or porter.

2 Service by post

Order 65, r 5(1)(*b*) provides for service of a document by post. The term 'by post' includes ordinary post, registered post and recorded delivery.

By the Interpretation Act 1978, s 7, where an Act authorises or requires any document to be served by post (whether the expression 'serve' or the expression 'give' or 'send' or any other expression is used) then, unless the contrary intention appears, service is deemed to be effected by properly addressing, pre-paying and posting a letter containing the document and, unless the contrary is proved, to have been effected by properly addressing, pre-paying and posting a letter containing the document and, unless the contrary is proved, to have been effected at the time at which the letter would be delivered in the ordinary course of post.

A document sent to an address with which the proposed recipient had had no connection for five months was not 'properly addressed' for the purposes of s 7 (*White* v *Weston* [1968] 2 QB 647).

Reference should be made to the notes on postal service in Chapter 1. It follows from the fact that service is deemed good that documents may frequently be properly served on parties who are temporarily away from their normal address. However, if the defendant subsequently applies to have judgment based on such service set aside, he may well have to pay the costs of that application thrown away (*Cooper* v *Scott-Farnell* [1969] 1 WLR 120). In that case the defendant was on holiday for over two months, and it would obviously have been prudent for him to have made arrangements for collecting mail during such a lengthy absence. If a letter before action had been received before departure, the matter clearly should be put in the hands of someone who can protect the defendant's interests while he is away.

The *Catherineholm* case (see Chapter 1, head 6) is also authority for the proposition that postal service at the registered office of a company is good where the company has changed its registered office but omitted to register the change.

The vagaries of the postal service have resulted in a doubling of the times when service by post is deemed to be effected. Master's Practice Direction No 41 [1985] 1 WLR 489 (which does not apply to the service of originating process under Ord 10, r 1(3), as to which see Chapter 1, head 6) provides that,

> To avoid uncertainty as to the date of the service it will be taken (subject to proof to the contrary) that delivery in the ordinary course of post was effected (a) in the case of first class mail, on the second working day after posting, (b) in the case of second class mail, on the fourth working day after posting. 'Working days' are Monday to Friday, excluding any bank holiday.

Affidavits of service must state whether the document was dispatched by first or second class mail, and if this omitted, second class mail will be assumed.

Where a particular statute specifies, for instance, that service of a document *may* be by registered post, the document may nevertheless be served personally (*Jarvis* v *Hemmings* [1912] 1 Ch 462), or by ordinary post provided it reaches the intended recipient (*Sharpley* v *Manly* (1942) 166 LT 44).

3 Service by document exchange

Ord 65, r 5(1)(*c*) permits service 'where the proper address for service includes a numbered box at a document exchange, by leaving the document at that document exchange or at a document exchange which transmits documents every business day to that document exchange'. The rule only applies to document exchanges for the time being approved by the Lord Chancellor: at present, approval has been given to all the document exchanges currently (or which may in the future be) run by (a) Britdoc Ltd of Hays Wharf, Guildford, Surrey, and (b) Northern Document Exchange Ltd of 9A Middlesborough Wharf, Depot Road, Middlesborough, Cleveland.

A document left at a document exchange is deemed (unless the contrary is proved) to have been served on the second business day following the day on which it is left (r 5(2A)). 'Business day' is defined as any day other than a Saturday, a Sunday, Christmas Day, Good Friday or a bank holiday under the Banking and Financial Dealings Act 1971 (r 5(3)).

4 Judgments and orders

Ordinarily, in the Queen's Bench Division, orders need not be served (*Farden* v *Richter* (1889) 23 QBD 124). Consequently, a money judgment may be enforced by a writ of fi fa even though the judgment or notice of it has not been served on the debtor *unless* the judgment or order directs payment within a specified time, in which case it must be served and service proved before the writ will issue.

The general rule does not apply to an order requiring a person to do, or refrain from doing, an act, which may be enforced under RSC Ord 45, r 5, once it has been served under RSC Ord 45, r 7. Subject to exceptions (see below), such an order may not, by r 7(2), be enforced unless:

(a) a copy of the order has been served personally on the person required to do or abstain from doing the act in question; and

(b) in the case of an order requiring a person to do an act, the copy has been so served before the expiration of the time within which he was required to do the act.

Where the order is made against a body corporate, r 7(3) provides that it cannot be enforced under Ord 45, r 5, unless:

(a) a copy of the order has also been served personally on the officer against whose property leave is sought to issue a writ of sequestration or against whom an order of committal is sought; and

(b) in the case of an order requiring the body corporate to do an act, the copy has been so served before the expiration of the time within which the body was required to do the act.

By r 7(4) there must be indorsed on the copy of the order served a penal notice informing the recipient:

(a) in the case of service on an individual, that if he neglects to obey the order within the time specified therein, or, if the order is to abstain from doing an act, that if he disobeys the order, he is liable to process of execution to comple him to obey it, and

(b) in the case of service on a body corporate (under r 7(3)), that if the body corporate neglects to obey the order within the time so specified or, if the order is to abstain from doing an act, that if the body corporate disobeys the order, he is liable to process of execution to compel the body to obey it.

Notice must be given of time for obedience, and thus with the copy of an order required to be served under r 7, being an order requiring a person to do an act, there must also be served a copy of any order under Ord 3, r 5, extending or abridging the time for doing the act and, where the first-mentioned order was made under Ord 45, rr 5(3) or 6 (specifying the time for obedience), a copy of the previous order requiring the act to be done (r 7(5)).

There are certain exceptions to personal service:

(1) An order requiring a person to abstain from doing an act may be enforced under Ord 45, r 5, if the court is satisfied that, even though it has not yet been served, the defendant has had notice of it either by being present when the order was made, or by being notified of the terms of the order, whether by telephone, telegram or otherwise.

(2) Orders for discovery or production of documents (under Ord 24, r 16(3)) and orders to answer interrogatories (under Ord 26, r 6(3)) are exempted by Ord 45, r 7(2), from the requirement of personal service, where the party's solicitor is served. In each case, though, the party may show on the application for his committal that he had no knowledge or notice of the order.

(3) Substituted service under Ord 65, r 4, may be ordered (see Chapter 7) and there is specific power in r 7(7) to dispense with service of the order if the court thinks it just to do so.

Where an undertaking is given to the court, service of the order recording the undertaking is not required prior to enforcement proceedings being started (*Hussain* v *Hussain* [1986] Fam 134).

Where an order is made against two or more parties jointly and severally liable, and one of them cannot be served, service against the other is sufficient to found a committal against the latter (*Re Ellis* (1906) 54 WR 526).

In the Chancery Division, once the draft of an order (having been drawn up by the registrar) is ready for perusal by the persons to do so, the registrar sends it to each of those persons together with all relevant documents. Where a party is acting by solicitors, the documents are sent by ordinary post and when acting in person, by registered post. The engrossment or duplicate of an order is similarly sent by post. When a draft, engrossment or duplicate is sent with a deed, probate or other document, it is always sent by registered post; see *Practice Direction* [1961] 1 WLR 47.

By RSC Ord 44, r 2(1), where in an action for the administration of the estate of a deceased person, or the execution of a trust, or the sale of any property, the court gives a judgment which affects the rights or interests of persons not parties to the action or directs any account to be taken or inquiry made, the court may, when giving the judgment or at any stage of the proceedings under the judgment direct notice of the judgment to be served on any such person. Subject to the person served applying within one month of service applying to discharge, vary or add to the judgment (under r 2(4)), he shall be bound by the judgment. The court may dispense with service if it appears to be impracticable, and may also order that such person be bound by the judgment (r 2(2)). Every notice of judgment for service under r 2 must be indorsed with a memorandum in Form 52A in Appendix A and accompanied by an acknowledgement of service in Form 15 with appropriate modifications (r 2(3)). A person served with notice of a judgment may, after acknowledging service of the notice, attend the proceedings after the judgment. Ord 12, rr 1 to 4 apply in relation to the acknowledgement of service, mutatis mutandis (r 2(6)).

In proceedings for the administration under the direction of the court of the estate of a deceased person or for the execution under the direction of the court of a trust, the court may direct an inquiry of debts and liabilities (Ord 44, r 4). By Ord 44, r 8, the court shall give directions that there be served on every creditor whose claim or any part thereof has been allowed or disallowed, and who did not attend when the claim was disposed of, a notice informing him of that fact.

An injunction must be drawn up etc as any other order in the Chancery Division. The person may only be committed once he has had actual notice of the order. Similar principles apply here as in the Queen's Bench Division (see also the *Supreme Court Practice*, para 45/7/7).

5 Orders for examination of judgment debtor

An order under RSC Ord 48, r 1, must be served personally on the judgment debtor and on any officer of a body corporate ordered to attend for examination (r 1(2)).

A penal notice must be served together with the order. Where the existence of the order is proved to have come to the debtor's knowledge (eg, because he was in court when it was made) *and* where he is evading service, the order may be enforced by committal.

In *Beeston Shipping Ltd* v *Babanaft International SA* [1985] 1 All ER 923, the Court of Appeal held that if the original date for the examination is adjourned, the judgment debtor will not be in contempt unless he is personally served with an amended order indorsed with the new date and a fresh penal notice. The knowledge of the debtor's legal representatives of the hearing date is not sufficient.

6 Orders to carry on proceedings

An order made under Ord 15, r 7, to continue proceedings after the death or bankruptcy of a party must be served on every other person who is a party to the cause or matter or who becomes or ceases to be a party by virtue of the order. Where a person becomes a defendant by virtue of the order, there must also be served on him a copy of the writ or originating summons by which the cause or matter was begun and a form of acknowledgement of service in Form 14 or 15 in Appendix A as appropriate (r 7(4)).

Where a person is made a defendant by virtue of an order under r 7, he is bound to acknowledge service (r 8(4)). The order served on him should contain the following notice or indorsement (*Supreme Court Practice*, para 15/7/23):

Take notice that from the time of the service of this order upon you, you will be bound by the proceedings in the action and that you should within 14 days of the service of the order upon you counting the day of service, return to the Court Office mentioned in this order the accompanying acknowledgement of service stating therein whether you intend to contest the proceedings, and that in default of you doing so the plaintiff may proceed in the action in your absence.

7 Subpoenas

By Ord 38, r 17, a writ of subpoena must be served personally and, subject to r 19, the service shall not be valid unless effected within twelve weeks after the date of issue and not less than four days or such other period as the court may fix, before the day on which attendance before the court is required.

Rule 19 deals with writs of subpoena in aid of an inferior court or tribunal. The Crown Office issues the writ without the need for a court order. It must also be served personally (r 19(3)) and must be served not less than four days before attendance is required (or such other period as the court may fix).

8 Notices of motion to commit

An application by motion to a Divisional Court for an order for committal (under Ord 52, r 1) after leave has been granted under r 2 must be served personally on the person sought to be committed. The notice of motion accompanied by a copy of the statement and affidavit in support of the application for leave must be served (r 3). Substituted service (see Chapter 6) may be ordered, or the court may dispense with service if it is just to do so (r 3(4)). At least eight clear days must be given between service and the hearing date (r 3(1)).

Furthermore, where a new or adjourned date is fixed for the hearing of the notice of motion, notification of that date ought to be by personal service (*Phonographic Performance Ltd* v *Tsang* (1985) 82 LSG 2331).

An application for committal to any other court is made by motion, supported by an affidavit and both documents must be served personally on the person sought to be committed (Ord 52, r 14). The court has a similar power to order substituted service or dispense with it (r 4(3)). See also Ord 45, r 7 (see head 3 above).

9 Charging orders

The service of notice of an order has to show cause after an application for a charging order has been made is governed by Ord 50, r 2. Rule 2(1) provides that, on the making of an order to show cause, notice of the order must, unless the court otherwise directs, be served as follows:

(*a*) a copy of the order, together with a copy of the affidavit in support, must be served on the judgment debtor;

(*b*) where the order relates to securities other than securities in court, copies of the order must also be served:

  (i) in the case of government stock for which the Bank of England keeps the register, on the Bank of England;

  (ii) in the case of government stock to which (i) does not apply, on the keeper of the register;

  (iii) in the case of stock of any body incorporated within England and Wales, on that body, or, where the register is kept by the Bank of England, on the Bank of England;

  (iv) in the case of stock incorporated outside England and Wales or of any state or territory outside the United Kingdom, being stock registered in a register kept in England and Wales, on the keeper of the register;

  (v) in the case of units of any unit trust in respect of which a register of the unit holders is kept in England and Wales, on the keeper of the register;

(*c*) where the order relates to a fund in court, a copy of the order must be served on the Accountant General at the Court Funds Office; and

(*d*) where the order relates to an interest under a trust, copies
of the order must be served on such of the trustees as the
court may direct.

Without prejudice to r 4(1), the court may, on making the order
to show cause, direct the service of copies of the order, and of the
affidavit in support, on any creditor of the judgment debtor or on
any other interested person as may be appropriate in the
circumstances (r 4(2)).

Documents to be served under r 4 must be served at least seven
days before the time appointed for the further consideration of the
matter (r 4(3)).

An application by a judgment creditor of a partner under Ord
81, r 10(1), for an order under the Partnership Act 1890, s 23, or
an application by a partner of the judgment debtor made in
consequence of the first-mentioned application, is made by
summons. The summons by the judgment creditor, and every
order made on the summons, must be served on the judgment
debtor and on such of his partners as are within the jurisdiction or,
if the partnership is a cost book company, on the judgment debtor
and the purser of the company (r 10(3)). The summons by the
partner, and every order made on the summons, must be served
on the judgment creditor, on the judgment debtor, and on such of
the other partners of the judgment debtor as do not join in the
application and are within the jurisdiction or, if the partnership is a
cost book company, on the purser of the company (r 10(4)).

Further, by r 10(5), a summons or order served under r 10 on
the purser of a cost book company or, in the case of a partnership
not being such a company, on some only of the partners thereof, is
deemed to have been served on that company or on all the
partners of that partnership, as the case may be.

10 Summonses

Applications in chambers are normally made by summons under
Ord 32. The service of a summons must, unless the court orders
otherwise or a rule provides otherwise, be served on every other
party not less than two clear days before the day specified in the
summons for the hearing thereof. However, where the summons
asks only for the extension or abridgement of a period of time, it
may be served on the day before the hearing date (Ord 32, r 3).

A summons for directions under Ord 25, r 1, is returnable in not
less than fourteen days after being taken out and should be served

promptly on the defendant so that he may be given fourteen days in which to specify his requirements and prepare for the hearing. If the defendant does not turn up to the hearing, the plaintiff must draw up and serve the order on him.

A summons for an interim payment under Ord 29, r 10, or for summary judgment under RSC Ord 14, r 1 (plus the affidavit in support and exhibits) must be served on the defendant not less than ten clear days before the return day (Ord 29, r 10(4) and Ord 14, r 2(3)).

An affidavit in reply to an Ord 14 summons should be served not less than three days before the hearing (Practice Direction (Order 14: Return date) [1970] 1 WLR 258).

Where, under RSC Ord 32, r 15 a Chancery master issues a summons requiring a person to attend before him as a witness, the summons must be served personally (r 15(2)).

An application by summons under the Arbitration Act 1979, s 1(5), must be served on the arbitrator or umpire and on any other party to the reference.

A summons in the Chancery Division under RSC Ord 92, r 5, to deal with money in court must be served on those persons who appear from the heading of the account to be entitled to the fund, or they should be made applicants. Where the amount in court is small and the parties numerous, service may be dispensed with (*Re Hodges* (1858) 6 WR 487, where it was felt that twenty-three grandchildren would be informed of the outcome by their parents who were served).

11 Notices of change of solicitor

A party giving notice of change of solicitor (having filed the notice in accordance with Ord 67, r 1(2)), must serve on every other party to the cause or matter (not being a party in default as to acknowledgement of service) and on the former solicitor a copy of the notice indorsed with a memorandum stating that the notice has been duly filed in the appropriate office (naming it) (r 1(3)).

12 Notices of appeal

A notice of appeal must be served on all parties to the proceedings in the court below who are directly affected by the appeal (Ord 59, r 3(5)). Subject to Ord 59, r 8, it is not necessary to serve the notice on parties not so affected.

Order 59, r 8(1) provides that the Court of Appeal or a single judge or the registrar may in any case direct that a notice of appeal or respondent's notice be served on any party to the proceedings in the court below on whom it has not been served, or on any person not party to those proceedings.

Where such a direction is given, the hearing of the appeal may be postponed or adjourned for such period and on such terms as may be just, and such judgment may be given and such order made on the appeal as might have been given or made if the persons served in pursuance of the direction had originally been parties (r 8(2)).

Generally, every notice of appeal must be served not later than four weeks after the date on which the judgment or order of the court below was sealed or otherwise perfected (Ord 59, r 4(1)).

Where leave to appeal is required, a valid notice of appeal can only be served after leave is granted. Where leave to appeal is granted by the Court of Appeal upon an application made within the time limited for serving notice of appeal under r 4(1), a notice of appeal may, instead of being served within that time, be served within seven days after the date when leave is granted (r 4(3)).

In an appeal from the county court, the notice of appeal must also be served on the registrar (Ord 59, r 19(2), and time for appealing runs from the date of the judgment or order of the county court (r 19(3)).

In an appeal against a decree nisi of divorce or nullity, the notice of appeal must also be served on the appropriate registrar, and time for appealing runs from the date on which the decree was pronounced.

In an appeal from Social Security Commissioners, the notice of appeal must be served within six weeks from the date on which notice of the Commissioners' grant or refusal of leave was given in writing to the appellant and must also be served on the Secretary of State and any person appointed by him to proceed with a claim (r 21).

A respondent's notice must be served on the appellant and on all parties to the proceedings in the court below who are directly affected by the contentions of the respondent, and must be served within 21 days after the service of the notice of appeal on the respondent (r 6(3)).

The time for serving notice of appeal may be extended by the court below if an application is made (but not necessarily heard) before the expiration of the period (Ord 59, r 15). Once the period has expired, the application for an extension must be made to the Court of Appeal (the Registrar of Civil Appeals or, where leave to appeal is also sought, to a single Lord Justice). The application is made by summons, under r 14(1), giving the other side at least seven days' notice. It must be supported by affidavit. The exercise of the Court of Appeal's discretion in such an application is discussed in the Supreme Court Practice para 59/4/4.

Chapter 4

High Court Pleadings

The rules as to service of pleadings in the High Court are contained in RSC Ord 18, rr 1–5.

1 Statements of claim

Order 18, r 1, provides that, unless the court gives leave to the contrary or a statement of claim is endorsed on the writ, the plaintiff must serve a statement of claim on the defendant or, if there are two or more defendants, on each defendant, and must do so either when the writ is served on that defendant or at any time after service of the writ but before the expiration of fourteen days after that defendant gives notice of intention to defend.

Subject to an exception, if the defendant does not give notice of intention to defend, there is no need for the plaintiff to serve a statement of claim on him. The exception is where the plaintiff wishes to proceed against the defendant and the writ is indorsed with a claim other than a claim for a liquidated demand, or unliquidated damages, or for the return of goods or the recovery of land. Here, the plaintiff should serve a statement of claim and continue the action as if the defendant had given notice of intention to defend.

The time limit may be extended or abridged either by order of the court or with the written consent of the parties (Ord 3, r 5). This applies to all pleadings and it is common practice to consent to a request for a reasonable extension, thus avoiding the additional costs of a court application.

Where a person fails to serve a statement of claim in time, the defendant may apply to the court for an order to dismiss the action under Ord 19, r 1.

The fourteen-day period after notice of intention to defend has been given does not run during August (Ord 3, r 3). Further, by Ord 18, r 5, neither the statement of claim nor any other pleading must be served during August without the leave of the court or with the consent of all the parties. However, this rule does *not* apply to a statement of claim indorsed on the writ (*Murray* v *Stephenson* (1887) 19 QBD 60). If the statement of claim is served during August this is an irregularity which may be remedied under Ord 2 (*MacFoy* v *United Africa Co* [1962] AC 152).

By Ord 65, r 7, if the statement of claim is served after 4 pm on Monday–Friday, service is deemed to have taken place on the following day; and if it is served after noon on Saturday, service is deemed to have taken place on the following Monday.

The provision that each defendant must be served with a statement of claim may be relaxed where they are each represented by the same solicitor, or where there are many defendants, differently represented or in person, and a large quantity of documents may be distributed needlessly. In the latter case an application should be made by the plaintiff for suitable directions.

If the plaintiff wishes not to serve a statement of claim, he may apply by summons to a master for leave to dispense with service. Such an application may be made where the action is suitable for trial without pleadings (Ord 18, r 21) or in some building contract cases to be tried by an official referee.

2 Defences

Order 18, r 2(1), provides that, subject to r 2(2), a defendant who gives notice of intention to defend an action must, unless the court gives leave to the contrary, serve a defence on the plaintiff before the expiration of fourteen days after the time limited for acknowledging service of the writ or after the statement of claim is served on him, whichever is the later. Since 'the time limited for acknowledging service of the writ' is, generally, fourteen days after service, this rule gives a defendant twenty-eight days from service of the writ to serve his defence, even if the statement of claim is served with the writ. However, where the statement of claim is served more than fourteen days after the writ is served, the defendant has fourteen days from service of the statement of claim to serve his defence.

Where the time limited for acknowledging service expires on a day when the Court Offices are closed, but service is acknowledged on the next day when they are open, the time for serving the defence starts to run from the later day (Ord 3, r 4).

For extension of the time limit, see under Statement of Claim.

The court has power to give leave to dispense with service of a defence. The defendant should take out a summons setting out his reasons and asking that service of his defence may be deferred or dispensed with. Examples of reasons for making the application are:

 (a) where the action is one which does not require any further pleading after the statement of claim, under RSC Ord 18, r 21;

 (b) when the defendant wishes to apply for security for costs on the ground that the plaintiff is out of the jurisdiction, under RSC Ord 23;

 (c) where the defendant wishes to apply to strike out the statement of claim, under Ord 18, r 19 (*Attorney-General of the Duchy of Lancaster* v *London and North Western Railway Company* [1892] 3 Ch 274); and

 (d) where the defendant wishes to apply for further and better particulars of the statement of claim before serving his defence, under Ord 18, r 12(5).

Where there is more than one defendant, each should serve a separate defence if their defences are not identical, or if they wish to be represented by different counsel at the trial.

In relation to summonses for summary judgment, Ord 18, r 2(2) provides that if a summons under Ord 14, r 1, or under Ord 86, r 1, is served on a defendant before he serves his defence, r 2(1) does not have effect in relation to him unless by the order made on the summons he is given leave to defend the action and, in that case, has effect as if it required him to serve his defence within fourteen days after the making of the order or within such other period as may be specified.

Where a summons for summary judgment is served the defendant ought not to serve his defence until the summons is heard (*Hobson* v *Monks* [1884] WN 8).

3 Counterclaims against non-parties

Where a person other than the plaintiff is joined in a counterclaim under Ord 15, r 3, the counterclaim must be served on him and, if he is not already a party to the action, a form of acknowledgement of service (Form 14 in Appendix A) must also be served. He then becomes a party from the time of service, and the counterclaim is treated in the same way as if it were a writ.

A counterclaim against a person who is already a party must be served within the same time limit as a defence must be served on the plaintiff under Ord 18, r 2 (see above) (Ord 15, r 3(3)).

4 Replies and defences to counterclaims

By Ord 18, r 3(4), a reply must be served by the plaintiff (where one is needed) before the expiration of fourteen days after service of the defence on him, and the same time limit applies to service of a defence to counterclaim. Where, as often happens, a reply and defence to counterclaim are both served by the plaintiff, they must be included in the same document (Ord 18, r 3(3)).

A counterclaim by a defendant is treated in the same way as a claim by a plaintiff, so that a defence to it must be served by the plaintiff if he intends to defend it (Ord 18, r 3(2)). If the plaintiff does not serve a reply (where Ord 18, r 8 does not require one) then he will be taken to have joined issue with the defence under Ord 18, r 14(1) (Ord 18, r 3(1)).

In certain admiralty actions the court's leave must be obtained before a reply or defence to counterclaim may be served (see Ord 75, r 20).

5 Further pleadings

By Ord 18, r 4, no pleading subsequent to a reply or defence to counterclaim shall be served except with the leave of the court.

Subsequent pleadings are rejoinder (by defendant), surrejoinder (by plaintiff), rebutter (by defendant) and surrebutter (by plaintiff). There is very rarely any need to use them. An application for leave to serve one of these pleadings must be made on notice (*Monck v Smythe* [1895] 1 Ir R 200). It may be made either by summons to a Master or at the summons for directions or notice thereunder. The proposed pleading should be produced at the hearing. Leave will only be granted where the pleading is genuinely required to raise matters which must be pleaded. It will be refused where, for instance, the rejoinder merely repeats the substance of the defence.

For service in the Long Vacation, and extensions of time limits, see under Statement of claim (head 1 above).

A third party notice is served in the same way as, and as if it was, a writ (Ord 16, r 3).

Chapter 5

Specific Defendants

This chapter deals with service of High Court documents on certain specific defendants, where the RSC, in conjunction with relevant statutes, prescribe procedures governing service.

1 The Crown, ministers etc

The procedure governing service on the Crown is contained in Ord 77, r 4, and the Crown Proceedings Act 1947, s 18. Orders 10, 11, and any other provision in the RSC relating to service out of the jurisdiction do *not* apply (Ord 77, r 4(1)).

Order 77, r 4(2), provides that personal service of any document required to be served on the Crown for the purpose of or in connection with any civil proceedings is not requisite; but where the proceedings are by or against the Crown service on the Crown must be effected:

  (*a*) by leaving the document at the office of the person who is, in accordance with the Crown Proceedings Act 1947, s 18, to be served, or of any agent who that person has nominated for the purpose, but in either case with a member of the staff of that person or agent, or

  (*b*) by posting it in a prepaid envelope addressed to the person who is to be served as aforesaid or to any such agent as aforesaid.

Section 18 of the Crown Proceedings Act 1947 provides that all documents required to be served on the Crown for the purpose of or in connection with any civil proceedings by or against the Crown must, if those proceedings are by or against an authorised government department, be served on the solicitor, if any, for that department, or the person, if any, acting for the purposes of the Act as solicitor for that department, or if there is no such solicitor and no person so acting, or if the proceedings are brought by or against the Attorney-General, on the Treasury Solicitor.

Furthermore, s 17 of the 1947 Act provides that the Treasury must publish a list of all the government departments and the names and addresses of their respective solicitors. The following list was published by the Treasury on 7 April 1979:

List of Authorised Government Departments for the purpose of Service of Documents

Authorised Government Department	*Solicitors and Addresses for Service*
Advisory, Conciliation and Arbitration Service	The Treasury Solicitor
	Queen Anne's Chambers
Board of Trade	28 Broadway
Ministry of Defence	Westminster
Department of Education and Science	London SW1H 9JS
Department of Employment	
Employment Service Agency	
Department of Energy	
Department of the Environment[1]	
Export Credits Guarantee Department	
Director General of Fair Trading	
Director General of Telecommunications	
Registry of Friendly Societies	
Health and Safety Commission	
Health and Safety Executive	
Department of Health and Social Security[2]	
Home Office	
Management and Personnel Office	
Manpower Services Commission	
Department for National Savings	
Northern Ireland Office	
Office of Arts and Libraries	
Public Works Loan Board	

Authorised Government Department	*Solicitors and Addresses for Service*
Office of Population Censuses and Surveys HM Stationery Office Department of Trade and Industry Training Services Agency Department of Transport HM Treasury Welsh Office[3]	The Treasury Solicitor Queen Anne's Chambers 28 Broadway Westminster London SW1H 9JS
Ministry of Agriculture, Fisheries and Food[3] Forestry Commissioners Intervention Board for Agricultural Produce	The Solicitor to the Ministry of Agriculture, Fisheries and Food 55 Whitehall London SW1A 2EY
Commissioners of Customs and Excise	The Solicitor for the Customs and Excise King's Beam House Mark Lane London EC3R 7HE
Commissioners of Inland Revenue	The Solicitor of Inland Revenue Somerset House London WC2R 1LB

Notes

(1) The solicitor for service in connection with the matters transferred from the Land Commission by the Land Commission (Dissolution) Act 1971, s 1(3) is the Solicitor to the Department of the Environment.

(2) The solicitor for service in connection with matters described hereunder is the Solicitor to the Department of Health and Social Security:

    (i) adjudications under legislation governing war pensions and social security (including child benefit, family income supplement and supplementary benefit) by the Secretary of State, a tribunal or other adjudicating authority;

    (ii) recovery of moneys under and matters arising from non-receipt of benefit under the legislation mentioned in sub-paragraph (i) above and cases stated under the Magistrates'

Courts Act 1980, s 111 in connection with prosecutions under such legislation; and

(iii) determinations by the Occupational Pensions Board.

The Treasury Solicitor is the solicitor acting for the Department of Health and Social Security in all other civil proceedings affecting that department.

(3) The solicitor for service in connection with the following matters is the Solicitor to the Ministry of Agriculture, Fisheries and Food: matters transferred from the Minister of Agriculture, Fisheries and Food to the Secretary of State for Wales by the Secretary of State for Wales and Minister of Land and Natural Resources Order 1965 (SI 1965 No 319), the Transfer of Functions (Wales) Order 1969 (SI 1969 No 388) or the Transfer of Functions (Wales) (No 1) Order 1978 (SI 1978 No 272). The Treasury Solicitor is the solicitor acting for the Welsh Office in all other civil proceedings affecting that office.

By RSC Ord 65, r 6, where documents are to be served on the Minister of a government department, or on the department itself, or on the Attorney-General, the procedure for service on the Crown (above) applies as it applies to service of proceedings on the Crown.

2 Members of the armed forces

The procedure governing service on members of the armed forces is set out in the following Memorandum issued by the Lord Chancellor's Office on 26 July 1979:

Memorandum on Service of Legal Process on Members of Her Majesty's Forces

Part 1: Preliminary

(1) This memorandum has been prepared for the information of solicitors who may wish, on behalf of their clients, to serve legal process in civil proceedings in the courts of England or Wales on parties to the proceedings who are (or who, at the material time, were) regular members of Her Majesty's Forces. It replaces an earlier memorandum on the same subject issued in December 1974.

(2) The legal process to which this memorandum relates includes process of the county court as well as the High Court, and includes interlocutory process as well as originating process. Proceedings for divorce or maintenance and proceedings in the Family Division generally are subject to special rules as to service which are explained in a practice direction issued by the Senior Registrar on 26th June 1979.

(3) For brevity, the client on whose behalf the solicitor desires to effect

service is referred to in this memorandum as the 'plaintiff' and the person to be served is referred to as the 'serviceman'; the expression 'overseas' means outside the United Kingdom.

Part 2: Enquiries as to Address

(4) As a first step, the plaintiff's solicitor will need to find out where the serviceman is serving, if he does not already know. For this purpose he should write to the appropriate office of the Ministry of Defence as specified in paragraph 10, below. In the case of a soldier (Other Ranks) in the Army the plaintiff's solicitor may need first to obtain a list of the Regiments and of the various Manning and Record Offices, in order to discover the appropriate office. He should write, sending a stamped addressed envelope, to the Officer in Charge, Central Clearing Wing, Higher Barracks, Exeter EX4 ND and a list will be supplied.

(5) The letter of enquiry should in every case show that the writer is a solicitor and that the enquiry is made solely with a view to the service of legal process in civil proceedings.

(6) In all cases the letter should give the full name, service number, rank or rating, and Ship, Arm or Trade, Regiment or Corps and Unit or so much of this information as is available. Failure to quote the service number and the rank or rating may result in failure to identify the serviceman or at least in considerable delay.

(7) The letter should contain an undertaking by the solicitor that, if the address is given, it will be used solely for the purpose of issuing and serving process in the proceedings and that so far as is possible the solicitor will disclose the address only to the Court and not to his client or to any other person or body. A solicitor in the service of a public authority or private company should undertake that the address will be used solely for the purpose of issuing and serving process in the proceedings and that the address will not be disclosed so far as possible to any other part of his employing organisation or to any other person but only to the Court. Normally on receipt of the required information and undertaking the appropriate office will give the service address.

(8) If the solicitor does not give the undertaking, the only information he will receive will be whether the serviceman is at that time serving in England or Wales, Scotland, Northern Ireland or overseas.

(9) It should be noted that a serviceman's address which ends with a British Forces Post Office address and reference (BFPO) will nearly always indicate that he is serving overseas.

(10) The letter of enquiry should be addressed as follows:

(*a*)	Officers of Royal Navy and Women's Royal Naval Service	Ministry of Defence Naval Secretary Old Admiralty Building Whitehall London SW1A 2BD

	Ratings in the Royal Navy WRNS Ratings QARNNS Ratings	The Commodore (Naval Drafting Division) HMS Centurion Grange Road Gosport Hants PO13 9XA
	RN Medical and Dental Officers	Ministry of Defence Medical Director General (Naval) First Avenue House High Holborn London WC1V 6HE
	Officers of Queen Alexandra's Royal Naval Nursing Service	Ministry of Defence The Matron-in-Chief QARNNS First Avenue House High Holborn London WC1V 6HE
	Naval Chaplains	Ministry of Defence Chaplain of the Fleet Lacon House Theobalds Road London WC1T 8RY
(b)	Royal Marine Officers	The Commandant- General Royal Marines MS Branch Old Admiralty Building Whitehall London SW1A 2BE
	Royal Marine Ranks	The Commodore (DRORM) HMS Centurion Grante Road Gosport Hants PO13 9XA
(c)	Army Officers (including WRAC and QARANC)	Ministry of Defence Army Officer's Documentation Office Government Buildings F Block Stanmore Middlesex HA7 4PZ

Soldiers (other ranks) Army (including WRAC and QARANC)	The Manning and Record Office which is appropriate to the Regiment or Corps
(*d*) Royal Air Force and Women's Royal Air Force Officers (including PMRAFNS)	Ministry of Defence AR8b (RAF) Eastern Avenue Barnwood Gloucester GL4 7PN
Airmen and Airwomen (other ranks)	Ministry of Defence RAF Personnel Management Centre RAF Innsworth Gloucester GL3 1EZ

Part 3: Assistance in Serving Proceedings on Servicemen

(11) Once the plaintiff's solicitor has learnt the servicemen's address, he may use that address as the address for service by post, in cases where this method of service is allowed by Rules of Court. With regard to proceedings in the county court, certain other methods of effecting service are provided; solicitors are referred, in particular, to CCR Order 8, Rules 17 and 18 [*now repealed by the County Court Rules 1981*]. There are, however, some situations in which service of the proceedings, whether in the High Court or in the county court, has to be effected personally; in these cases an appointment will have to be sought, through the Commanding Officer of the Unit, Establishment or Ship concerned, for the purpose of effecting service. The procedure for obtaining an appointment is described below, and it applies whether personal service is to be effected by the plaintiff's solicitor or his agent or by a court bailiff, or, in the case of proceedings served overseas (with the leave of the court), through the British Consul or the foreign judicial authority.

(12) The procedure for obtaining an appointment to effect personal service is by application to the Commanding Officer of the Unit, Establishment or Ship in which the serviceman is serving. The Commanding Officer may grant permission for the process server to enter the Unit, Establishment or Ship but if this is not appropriate he may offer arrangements for the serviceman to attend at a place in the vicinity of the Unit, Establishment or Ship in order that he may be served. If suitable arrangements cannot be made the solicitor will have evidence that personal service is impracticable, which may be useful in an application for substituted service.

Part 4: General

    (13) Subject to the procedure outlined in paragraphs 11 and 12, there are no special arrangements to assist in the service of process when a serviceman is outside the United Kingdom. The appropriate office will however give an approximate date when the serviceman is likely to return to the United Kingdom.

    (14) It sometimes happens that a serviceman has left the service by the time that the enquiry is made. If the plaintiff's solicitor confirms that the proceedings result from an occurrence when the serviceman was in the Forces and he gives the undertaking referred to in paragraph 7, the last known private address after discharge will normally be provided. In no other case however will the Department disclose the private address of a member of HM Forces.

Members of US Air Force

The Lord Chancellor's Office, in conjunction with the approval of the United States authorities, has issued the following note to assist people wishing to bring claims against members of the United States Air Force serving in this country.

Instructions have been issued by the US authorities to the commanding officers of all their units in this country that every facility is to be given for the service of process on members of the US Air Force. The proper course to be followed by a creditor or other person having a claim against a member of the US Air Force is for him to communicate with the commanding officer or, where the unit concerned has a legal officer, with the legal officer of the defendant's unit requesting him to provide facilities for the service of process on the defendant. It is not possible for the US authorities to act as arbitrators when a civil claim in contract or tort is made against a member of their forces. It is, therefore, essential that the claim should either be admitted by the defendant or should be reduced to judgment, whether in the High Court or a county court. If a claim has been admitted or judgment has been obtained and the claimant has been unable to obtain satisfaction within a reasonable period, his proper course is then to write to: Office of the Staff Judge Advocate, Headquarters, Third Air Force, RAF Mildenhall, Suffolk, enclosing a copy of the defendant's written admission of the claim or, as the case may be, a copy of the judgment. Steps will be thereupon be taken by the Staff Judge Advocate to ensure that the matter is brought to the defendant's attention with a view to prompt satisfaction of the claim.

3 Partners

The service of a writ on a firm is governed by Ord 81, r 3. By r 3(1), where by virtue of Ord 81, r 1, partners are sued in the name of a firm, the writ may, except in the case mentioned in r 3(3), be served:

(*a*) on any one or more of the partners; or

(*b*) at the principal place of business of the partnership within the jurisdiction, on any person having at the time of service the control or management of the partnership business there; or

(*c*) by sending a copy of the writ by ordinary first-class post (as defined in Ord 10, r 1(2): see Chapter 1) to the firm at the principal place of business of the partnership within the jurisdiction,

and subject to r 3(2), where service of the writ is effected in accordance with this paragraph, the writ will be deemed to have been duly served on the firm, whether or not any member of the firm is out of the jurisdiction.

The rule applies only to a firm carrying on business within the jurisdiction (Ord 81, r 1). It is immaterial that all the partners reside and are domiciled out of the jurisdiction where, for example, the manager is served under r 3(1)(*b*) (see eg *Worcester City & County Banking Co* v *Firbank, Pauling & Co* [1894] 1 QB 784). Service on a partner who is temporarily within the jurisdiction is good service on the firm. However, if it is necessary to serve a partner personally, and he is out of the jurisdiction, he must be served under RSC Ord 11 (see Part II).

The 'principal place of business' means a place where the business of the firm is carried on in the firm's name by a partner or by another person in the firm's pay, though not just an agent. What constitutes the principal place of business where there are a number is a question of fact. A person having the 'control and management of the partnership business' does not include an employee who happens to be on the premises in the absence of the partners and manager, but must be someone exercising de facto control and management.

Where a writ is served under r 3(1)(*c*), r 3(2) provides that:

(*a*) the date of service will, unless the contrary is shown, be deemed to be the seventh day (ignoring Ord 3, r 2(5): see below) after the date on which the copy was sent to the firm; and

(*b*) any affidavit proving due service of the writ must contain a statement to the effect that:

(i) in the opinion of the deponent (or, if the deponent is the plaintiff's solicitor or an employee of that solicitor, in the opinion of the plaintiff) the copy of the writ, if sent to the firm at the address in question, will have

come to the knowledge of one of the persons mentioned para (*a*) or (*b*) within seven days; and
(ii) the copy of the writ has not been returned to the
plaintiff through the post undelivered to the addressee.

For affidavits of service, see Appendix 2, Forms 4 and 5.

Where, apart from this paragraph, the period in question, being
a period of seven days or less, would include a Saturday, Sunday
or bank holiday, Christmas Day or Good Friday, that day shall be
excluded. 'Bank holiday' means a day which is, or is to be
observed as, a bank holiday, under the Banking and Financial
Dealings Act 1971, in England and Wales (Ord 3, r 2(5)).

Order 81, r 3(3) provides that where a partnership has, to the
knowledge of the plaintiff, been dissolved before an action against
the firm is begun, the writ by which the action is begun must be
served on every person within the jurisdiction sought to be made
liable in the action.

A writ may be issued against a firm after its dissolution provided
the cause of action accrued beforehand (*In re Wenham* [1900] 2
QB 698). See also *Supreme Court Practice*, para 81/3/7.

Every person on whom a writ is served under Ord 81, r 3(1)(*a*)
or (*b*), must at the time of service be given a written notice stating
whether he is served as a partner or as a person having the control
or management of the partnership business or both as a partner
and as such a person; and any person on whom a writ is so served
but to whom no notice is given shall be deemed to be served as a
partner (Ord 81, r 3(4)). The notice should be in the form:

Take notice that the writ served herewith is served on you as
(i) the person having the control or management of the defendant firm
of Bloggins & Co [*and/or*
(ii) a partner in the defendant firm of Bloggins & Co]

See Form 6 in Appendix 2.

If the plaintiff omits to serve the notice when serving a person in
control of the business, it is open to the latter to deny that he was a
partner at the material time (and thus to avoid liability) in his
acknowledgement of service (Ord 81, r 4(2)).

Where more than one person is served in relation to a particular
firm, time for acknowledging service runs from the date of the last
of the services (*Alden* v *Beckley & Co* (1890) 25 QBD 543).

A firm not carrying on business within the jurisdiction cannot be
served under RSC Ord 11 in the firm's name, though it can validly
agree to accept service through an agent who is within the

jurisdiction. If it is sued in the firm's name, service on a partner within the jurisdiction is not good service on the firm (*Western National Bank of New York* v *Perez* [1891] 1 QB 304). The firm must be sued in the individual partners' names and must be served as ordinary defendants either within the jurisdiction or abroad under RSC Ord 11. See also the notes to RSC Ord 81, rr 1, 3 in the *Supreme Court Practice*.

4 Corporate bodies generally

Order 65, r 3(1) provides that personal service of a document on a body corporate may, in cases for which provision is not otherwise made by an enactment, be effected by serving it in accordance with Ord 65, r 2 (see Chapter 1, head 5) on the mayor, chairman or president of the body, or the town clerk, clerk, secretary, treasurer or other similar officer thereof.

Where a writ is served on a body corporate in accordance with Ord 10, r 1(2) (see Chapter 1, head 1), that rule has effect as if for the reference to the usual or last known address of the defendant there were substituted a reference to the registered or principal office of the body corporate and as if for the reference to the knowledge of the defendant there were substituted a reference to the knowledge of a person mentioned in r 3(1) (r 3(2)).

It is clear, therefore, that where a statute provides a method of service in the case of a particular body corporate, that method must be used. Where there is no such statutory provision, service may be effected by one of the methods described in this rule. Bodies subject to specific statutory rules as to service are dealt with under heads 5 and 6 below. Bodies not so subject are listed under head 7 below.

Note that the word 'clerk' in r 3 (1) means a principal officer, principal clerk, secretary of a company or such like, and not a minor employee like a station booking clerk (*Mackereth* v *Glasgow & SW Railway Co* (1873) LR 8 Exch 149; *Walton* v *Universal Salvage Co* (1847) 16 M&W 438).

5 Companies

(a) British companies

By the Companies Act 1985, s 725(1), a document may be served on a company by leaving it at or sending it by post to the registered office of the company. (For winding-up petitions, see Chapter 2, head 2).

Where a company registered in Scotland carries on business in England, the process of any court in England may be served on the company by leaving it at or sending it by post to the principal place of business of the company in England, addressed to the manager or other head officer in England of the company (s 725(2)).

Where process is served on a company under s 725(2), the person issuing out the process must send a copy by post to the registered office of the company (s 725(3)).

Note that a company regulated by the Companies Act 1948 whose registered office is situated in Scotland and which does not carry on business in England is served under s 725(1).

The term 'by post' in s 725(1) includes ordinary post (Interpretation Act 1978, s 7), registered post (*TO Supplies (London) Ltd* v *Jerry Creighton Ltd* [1952] 1 KB 42) and hence recorded delivery (Recorded Delivery Service Act 1962). Section 725 applies to companies formed or registered under former Acts (see Companies Act 1985, Part XXII).

(b) Channel Islands and Isle of Man companies

Companies incorporated in these places with a place of business in England or Scotland are required to deliver certain documents to the registrar of companies as if they were registered in England or Scotland (Companies Act 1985, s 699). Service of process on them is as for foreign corporations (see below), though in the case of Guernsey, Jersey, Alderney and Sark, service of English process is possible there (see Notice of 6 March 1961 at 105 SJ 288).

(c) Foreign corporations

Companies with are incorporated outside Great Britain (ie outside England, Wales and Scotland) but which establish a place of business within Great Britain, called oversea companies, are regulated by the Companies Act 1985, Pt XXIII, Chapter 1. Section 695 of the Act provides that any process or notice required to be served on an oversea company is sufficiently served if addressed to any person whose name has been delivered to the registrar under the provisions of Pt XXIII and left at or sent by post to the address which has been so delivered; provided that:

(*a*) where any such company makes default in delivering to the registrar the name and address of a person resident in Great Britain who is authorised to accept on behalf of the company service of process or notices; or

(*b*) if at any time all the persons whose names and addresses have been so delivered are dead or have ceased so to reside, or refuse to accept service on behalf of the company, or for any reason cannot be served.

A document may be served on the company by leaving it at or sending it by post to any place of business established by the company in Great Britain.

Oversea companies are required to deliver to the registrar of companies for registration (inter alia), the names and addresses of some one or more person resident in Great Britain authorised to accept on behalf of the company service of process and any notices required to be served on the company (s 691(1)(b)). Any alteration in those names and addresses must be notified to the registrar within a prescribed time (s 692).

If a writ is to be served on a foreign company abroad, under Ord 11 the writ should be served on the manager/head officer at the company's head office (see Part II).

If the foreign corporation is not registered in Britain under s 691, but is nevertheless 'resident' here, it may be served here if its 'agent' is served with the process. A number of authorities on this procedure are mentioned in the *Supreme Court Practice*, paras 65/3/12. However, the proviso to s 695 should be borne in mind, so that if a company has established a place of business in this country, it is not necessary to look further than that section.

An example of 'residence' is the Court of Appeal's decision in *Dunlop* v *Actien Gesellschaft* [1902] 1 KB 342. The defendants were a foreign corporation who made cars abroad. They hired a stand at the Crystal Palace to exhibit their wares (including a car allegedly infringing the plaintiffs' patent) for nine days. The stand was in the charge of a person employed as their representative and salesman. It was held that during the show the defendants were resident within the jurisdiction and could be served with a writ.

The question of what constitutes residence, and also what constitutes an agent is one of fact. As to an agent, the rule was laid down by Blackburn J in *Newby* v *Van Oppen* (1872) LR 7 QB 293 at p 296: 'The clerk or officer must be in the nature of a head officer, whose knowledge would be that of the corporation.'

In the interesting recent decision of *Rothmans* v *Saudi Arabian Airlines* [1981] QB 368 the Court of Appeal held that where a statute (here, the Carriage by Air Act 1961) provides a more stringent test than just 'residence' (here, the defendant had to be 'ordinarily resident'), the test under the statute supersedes the common law rule.

6 Friendly societies

The rules as to service are contained in the Friendly Societies Act 1974, s 103. Where proceedings are brought against the trustees of a registered society or branch, they 'may be sued in their proper names without any other description than the title of their office.' The trustees would then be served according to the rules for serving individuals (s 103(1)).

Where proceedings are brought by a member of the society (or a person claiming through a member) the society may be sued in the name, as defendant, 'of any officer or person who receives contributions or issues policies on behalf of the society or branch within the jurisdiction of the court in which the legal proceedings are brought with the addition of the words 'on behalf of the society or branch' (naming the same) (s 103(2)).

By s 103(4) the summons, writ, process or other proceeding to be issued to or against the officer or other person sued on behalf of a registered society or branch is sufficiently served:

(i) by personally serving that officer or other person; or
(ii) by leaving a true copy thereof at the registered office of the society or branch, or at any place of business of the society or branch within the jurisdiction of the court in which the proceeding is brought; or
(iii) if that office or place of business is closed, by posting the copy on the outer door of that office or place of business.

Where the document is not served as in s 103(4), service is effected by sending a copy of it in a letter sent by registered post or by the recorded delivery service addressed to the committee at the registered office of the society or branch and posted at least six days before any step is taken in the proceedings (s 103(5)).

7 Other corporate bodies

The following bodies, though there may be statutory provisions regulating them, are not subject to specific statutory rules as to service, and so service should be effected under Ord 65, r 3:

Building societies. Incorporated under the Building Societies Act 1986, they can be sued in the corporate name, but must be served under Ord 65, r 3.

Charitable institutions. Unincorporated, the treasurer or secretary etc, should be sued 'on behalf of' the charity (naming it) and served, *or* the charity should be sued in its name and the treasurer or secretary etc served at the head office. If served elsewhere than at the head office, a copy of the process should also be left at head office.

Clubs.   Unincorporated, they cannot be sued in the club name. It may be possible to bring proceedings against representative defendants under Ord 15, r 12.

Foreign banks.   In *Lhoneux* v *Hong Kong Bank* (1886) 33 ChD 446 it was held that service on the manager of the London agency of a bank established by an ordinance and having its head office in Hong Kong was good.

Industrial and provident societies.   Incorporated under the Industrial and Provident Societies Act 1965, s 3, they can be sued in the corporate name, but must be served under Ord 65, r 3.

Local government bodies.   By the Local Government Act 1972, the following bodies are constituted as bodies corporate though, as no method of service is specified, Ord 65, r 3 applies: county councils and district councils (s 2); parish councils (s 14); community councils (s 33).

Trade unions.   Though a trade union is not a body corporate, it may (other than in actions for tort) be sued in its own name (Trade Union and Labour Relations Act 1974, s 2). Service is in accordance with RSC Ord 65, r 3.

Trustees.   By the Trustee Act 1925, s 59, where in an action the court is satisfied that diligent search has been made for any person who, in the character of trustee, is made a defendant in any action, to serve him with a process of the court, and that he cannot be found, the court may hear and determine the action and give judgment against that trustee as if he had been duly served, or had entered an appearance in the action (now, acknowledged service), and had also appeared by his counsel and solicitor at the hearing. This is without prejudice to any interest he may have in the matters in question in the action other than as a trustee.

Other incorporated bodies

Where a body was incorporated prior to 1845 by Royal Charter or otherwise, if its articles of incorporation provide for service of documents, that provision should be followed. If there is no such provision, service is under Ord 65, r 3.

8 Persons under disability

Order 80, r 16, lays down the procedure for serving on infants or mental patients those documents which are required to be served personally or in accordance with Ord 10, r 1(2) (r 16(1)).

Subject to exceptions r 16(2) provides that the document must be served:

(a) in the case of an infant who is not also a patient, on his father or guardian or, if he has no father or guardian, on the person with whom he resides or in whose care he is; and

(b) in the case of a patient, on the person (if any) who is authorised under the Mental Health Act 1983, Pt VII, to conduct in the name of the patient or on his behalf the proceedings in connection with which the document is to be served or, if there is no person so authorised, on the person with whom he resides or in whose care he is.

The document must be served in the manner required by the rules with respect to such a document (ibid).

By virtue of r 16(4), certain documents must be served personally on the person under disability, unless the court otherwise orders. Those documents are:

(a) a judgment or order requiring the person to do, or refrain from doing, any act;

(b) a notice of motion or summons for the committal of the person; and

(c) a writ of subpoena against the person.

Note, however, that as an exception to (a), Ord 24, r 16(3), and Ord 26, r 6(3), provide respectively that an order for the discovery or inspection of documents or an order for interrogatories may be served on a person's solicitor, and this will be sufficient to found an application for committal of the person disobeying the order. It is unlikely that the court will dispense with personal service unless it is satisfied that the person under disability has or will have personal knowledge of what he is required to do, or refrain from doing.

Rule 16(3) provides that, notwithstanding anything in r 16(2), the court may order that a document which has been or is to be served on the person under disability or on a person other than a person mentioned in r 16(2) shall be deemed to be duly served on the person under disability.

An application is made by summons to a master and is supported by an affidavit proving the defendant's status as a person under disability and stating the reasons for making the application. For instance, in the case of a minor, that he is of a reasonable age (say, sixteen) and has no father or guardian, and that he has been served personally with the writ.

9 Agents of foreign principals

Order 10, r 2, provides a procedure for serving a writ on a principal living and carrying on a business abroad, but who entered into a contract through an agent living or carrying on business within the jurisdiction.

By r 2(1) the court may authorise service of a writ beginning an action relating to a contract to be effected on the agent instead of the principal where it is satisfied on an ex parte application that:

(*a*) the contract has been entered into within the jurisdiction with or through an agent who is either an individual residing or carrying on business within the jurisdiction or a body corporate having a registered office or a place of business within the jurisdiction;

(*b*) the principal for whom the agent was acting was at the time the contract was entered into and is at the time of the application neither such an individual nor such a body corporate; and

(*c*) at the time of the application either the agent's authority has not been determined or he is still in business relations with his principal.

The application is made ex parte by affidavit. In the Queen's Bench Division the affidavit should be left at the Masters' Secretary's Department and collected later once the Master's decision has been indorsed on it. In the Chancery Division the application is made by summons or motion. The principles to be applied are contained in a memorandum dated the 4 December 1920 (65 SJ 131) which is set out in the *Supreme Court Practice*, para 10/2/2.

The order authorising service on the agent must limit a time within which the defendant must acknowledge service (r 2(2)) and a copy of the order and the writ must be sent by post to the defendant at his foreign address (r 2(3)).

10 Foreign states

The service of a writ or other document instituting proceedings against a state is governed by the State Immunity Act 1978, s 12, which provides that the document is served 'by being transmitted through the Foreign and Commonwealth Office to the Ministry of Foreign Affairs of the State'. For the procedure, see Chapter 16, head 5.

Chapter 6

Proof of Service

Where a plaintiff wishes to take some step in an action but the defendant has failed to attend a hearing, or file a defence or in some other way has defaulted in the procedure, the plaintiff will have to prove that the defendant has been served with the document giving notice of the hearing, or the writ, or whatever, before he will be allowed to proceed.

1 Writs

In order for a plaintiff to enter judgment under Ord 13, r 1 (where the defendant has failed to give notice of intention to defend), there are three alternative ways of proving service of the writ (Ord 13, r 7(1)):

(a) where the defendant has acknowledged service on him of the writ;

(b) where an affidavit is filed by or on behalf of the plaintiff proving due service of the writ on the defendant; and

(c) where the plaintiff produces the writ indorsed by the defendant's solicitor with a statement that he accepts service of the writ on the defendant's behalf (see Chapter 1, head 1).

Where the defendant has not acknowledged service, the court may require proof of such failure (Ord 13, r 7(2)) and this will usually be done by a search for an acknowledgement of service, evidenced by a certificate indorsement from a court officer.

An affidavit of service of any document must state by whom the document was served, the day of the week and date on which it was served, where it was served and how (except as provided in Ord 10, r 1(3)(b) and Ord 81, r 3(2)(b) (see Chapter 5, head 3) (Ord 65, r 8)).

An affidavit of service of a writ must, by Ord 10, r 1(3)(*b*), contain a statement to the effect that;

(*a*) in the deponent's opinion (or, if the deponent is the plaintiff's solicitor or an employee of that solicitor, in the plaintiff's opinion) the copy of the writ, if sent to, or as the case may be inserted through the letter box for, the address in question will have come to the knowledge of the defendant within seven days thereafter; and

(*b*) in the case of service by post, the copy of the writ has not been returned to the plaintiff through the post undelivered to the addressee.

In the case of postal service, the affidavit must specify whether the document was sent by first or second class mail. If it does not specify first class mail, service is deemed to have been effected by second class mail (*Masters' Practice Direction No 41*: see Chapter 3, head 2). For forms of affidavits of service of writ, see Appendix 2, Forms 1–9.

The introduction of the use of ordinary post for the service of writs produced obvious dangers, and a safeguard procedure was therefore provided to protect defendants. Order 13, r 7(3) provides that where a writ is served by post under Ord 10, r 1(2)(*a*), and judgment under Ord 13 is subsequently entered, but later the copy writ is returned through the post undelivered to the addressee, the plaintiff must before taking any step or further step in the action or the enforcement of the judgment, either make a request for the judgment to be set aside on the ground that the writ has not been duly served, or apply to the court for directions.

By r 7(4), a request under r 7(3)(*a*) is made by producing to an officer of the office in which judgment was entered (and leaving with him for filing) an affidavit stating the relevant facts, and thereupon the judgment is set aside and the entry of the judgment and of any proceedings for its enforcement made in the book kept in the office for that purpose are marked accordingly.

The alternative course applies where the writ has been returned and the plaintiff suspects that the defendant has not genuinely gone away and is trying to evade service.

By r 7(5), the application under r 7(3)(*b*) is made ex parte by affidavit stating the facts on which the application is founded and any order or direction sought. The court may then:

(*a*) set aside judgment; or

(*b*) direct that, notwithstanding the return of the copy of the writ, it shall be treated as having been duly served; or (*c*) make such other order and give such other direction as the circumstances may require.

The court may, for instance, order the plaintiff to serve a summons on the defendant asking for the order/direction sought by him, to give the defendant a chance to state his side of the story.

2 Other documents

Where necessary, service of other documents is proved by an affidavit of service, forms of which are contained in Appendix 2.

Note that where a party does not appear at a hearing and an order is made against him, the order may be made even if an affidavit of service has not yet been filed. The order is usually made subject to an affidavit of service or the written acknowledgement of service. If the respondent appears, or does not appear but consents to an adjournment, and the summons is adjourned to a specified day and hour, no affidavit of service or notice is required. Otherwise, there must be an affidavit proving that the respondent had notice of the adjourned hearing in addition to an affidavit of the original service.

In the Chancery Division, an affidavit of service may be sworn and filed at any time before the drawing up of the order. If the affidavit is sworn after the date of the order, the order is not post-dated and the affidavit is not entered formally as evidence. The Registrar makes a memorandum in the margin of the order that the affidavit has been sworn and filed, and included in the order are the words, 'no one appearing for X, although duly served as by affidavit appears'. The same practice applies in the Queen's Bench Division: ie, the order must be dated the day it was pronounced, even when the affidavit is sworn later (see (1884) 28 SJ 541 and the *Supreme Court Practice*, para 42/3/3).

Service of a winding-up or bankruptcy petition is proved by affidavit, in the case of a winding-up petition specifying the manner of service (Insolvency Rules, rr 4.9, 6.15). The affidavit must exhibit a sealed copy of the petition and, if substituted service has been ordered, a sealed copy of the order. The affidavit is filed in court immediately after service (rr 4.9(2) and 6.15(2)).

Chapter 7

Substituted Service

It is sometimes not possible to serve a person personally with a document, for example, because he has disappeared or taken steps to avoid the process server. In such a case, RSC Ord 65, r 4, provides an alternative procedure for serving the document, called 'substituted service'. Rule 4(1) provides that if, in the case of any document which by virtue of any provision of these rules is required to be served personally or a document to which Ord 10, r 1 applies, it appears to the court that it is impracticable for any reason to serve the document personally on that person, the court may make an order for substituted service of that document.

1 The application

By r 4(2), an application for an order for substituted service may be made by an affidavit stating the facts on which the application is founded.

Before an application is made, strenuous efforts must be made to serve the recipient. The procedure recommended in the *Supreme Court Practice*, para 65/4/7 is as follows:

(1) Two calls should be made either at the defendant's residence (permanent or temporary) if known, or if the claim relates to the defendant's business, at his business address. If the defendant has left the address given on the writ, this should be stated in the affidavit (see below). If a copy of the document to be served is left, it must be in a sealed envelope addressed to the defendant.

(2) Each call should be on a weekday, and on a separate day, and at a reasonable hour.

(3) The second call should be made by appointment by a letter sent to the defendant by ordinary post, giving not less than

two clear days' notice, enclosing a copy of the document to be served, and offering an opportunity of making a different appointment.

(4) When the appointment is kept, the server should ask whether the defendant has received the letter of appointment with the copy document, and if he is told that the defendant is away, he should ask whether letters have been forwarded to an address within the jurisdiction. If so, the defendant may be shown to have received communications sent to him.

The affidavit (for which see Form 12 in Appendix 2) should state the following:

(a) that a writ has been issued (a copy should be exhibited and the date of issue given);

(b) the efforts that have been made to serve the document personally (following the procedure outlined above) and whether the letter of appointment was returned (any answer to it should be exhibited, as well as the document to be served);

(c) that all practicable means of effecting personal service have been exhausted;

(d) that the proposed method of substituted service will probably come to the defendant's knowledge;

(e) where applicable, that the defendant is evading service and the reasons for that belief; and

(f) that the defendant is, or is believed to be, within the jurisdiction.

In the Queen's Bench Division, the application is made ex parte to a master (or district registrar). The affidavit is left in the Masters' Secretary's Department (Room 120, RCJ) and collected from there with the master's decision indorsed on it. The order must be drawn up.

In the Chancery Division, the application is made ex parte and in a clear case is heard by a master (or district registrar). Otherwise it is referred to a judge. The order must be drawn up. An office copy of the affidavit need only be bespoken for use by the court or judge where either so direct. (In an action by a trustee in bankruptcy, no summons is necessary and the application is made ex parte to a master.)

In the Family Division the application is made ex parte to a Registrar and the order is drawn up officially.

An application for substituted service of a notice of motion to commit or for attachment is made to a judge in chambers and not to a master.

Where the document to be served is a writ, the need for substituted service has been drastically reduced since the abolition of the request for personal service. Where the defendant's address is known, he can be served by ordinary post under Ord 10, r 1, and substituted service by that method will generally be otiose and render the plaintiff liable in costs. However, there may be justification if the defendant was deliberately evading service and it was thought that he would maliciously return a letter marked 'gone away'.

In *Gurtner* v *Circuit* [1968] 2 QB 587 at p 605, the Court of Appeal held that, in a personal injury action arising out of a road accident, where the defendant is insured with a known insurance company, an order may be made for substituted service on the defendant at the insurers' address, if the writ is thereby likely to reach the defendant. Where the defendant's insurers are not known, or it seems he was uninsured, and the Motor Insurers' Bureau will be liable to pay damages, an order for substituted service may be made upon the defendant at the Motor Insurers' Bureau's address (ibid).

Recently, the Court of Appeal held that where the defendant in a personal injury case was avoiding service of the writ, it was not a pre-requisite of the court extending the validity of the writ after its expiry date for the plaintiff's solicitor to have attempted substituted service on the defendant's insurer. The defendant's elusiveness alone amounted to exceptional circumstances (*Siksnys* v *Hanley* (1982) *The Times*, 26 May).

2 The order

Where a master has refused to order substituted service, an appeal against the refusal is by ex parte application to a judge in chambers, and from him, with leave, ex parte to the Court of Appeal.

Where substituted service has been granted, the usual form that an order takes is service by letter or advertisement, though any other method which is likely to work is permissible. Order 65, r 4(3), provides that substituted service 'is effected by taking such steps as the court may direct to bring the document to the notice of the person to be served'. The order must be served together with the document. Once those steps have been taken, substituted service has 'all the effects of personal service' (*Watt* v *Barnett* (1878) 3 QBD 183 at p 186) and the defendant will only be permitted to defend if he can show a defence on the merits.

Substituted service will only be ordered where personal service could have been effected but for the difficulties. So it is not available where, for instance, the defendant is a foreign sovereign who could not have been personally served without first submitting to the jurisdiction (*Mighell* v *Sultan of Johore* [1894] 1 QB 149). Further, if a writ was issued for service within the jurisdiction, personal service must have been permissible at the date of issue ie, the defendant must then have been within the jurisdiction. If he was not, substituted service cannot normally be ordered.

However, if the defendant left the jurisdiction to evade service, substituted service may be ordered. Indeed, this rule applies even when it cannot be shown that the defendant's intention was to evade service, provided he left the jurisdiction after issue of the writ and with knowledge of its issue, if it would be 'just' so to order (*Jay* v *Budd* [1898] 1 QB 12). It would not be just where the absence was temporary and there was clearly no intention to evade service, eg, in the case of servicemen serving overseas. Nevertheless, the need for substituted service of writs has been greatly reduced (see above). The procedure for substituted service of writs out of the jurisdiction depends on whether the writ was issued for service within, or outside, the jurisdiction, see below.

3 Effecting service

Where the person to be served is an individual, substituted service will be ordered either on a person who is impliedly authorised to accept service of the document in question (eg a solicitor acting in respect of the subject matter of the action), or on a person who is at least likely to communicate the document to the individual.

Where no-one can be found who falls within either category, the court may order service by advertisement, for example, in a newspaper sold in the locality where the defendant is believed to live. There must always be good grounds for believing that the defendant will see the advertisement.

4 Proof of service

An affidavit of substituted service is needed. It must refer to the writ and the order for substituted service (see Appendix 2, Form 13). Where service was by advertisement, the affidavit must state the name and date of the paper and must either set out the advertisement or exhibit a copy of the paper.

Where service was by letter, the affidavit must state that the letter was prepaid. By *Masters' Practice Direction No 20*, para (6), unless the court otherwise directs, a copy of the order and of the writ is deemed to have been served on the day following the day on which a prepaid letter containing such copy was posted.

5 Service out of the jurisdiction

The procedure for substituted service out of the jurisdiction depends on whether the writ was issued for service within, or out of, the jurisdiction.

(a) Within

Where a writ was issued for service within the jurisdiction but the defendant is in fact outside the jurisdiction, leave to issue a concurrent writ for service out of the jurisdiction should be applied for under Ord 6, r 6. Leave should also be sought to serve the writ outside the jurisdiction. If it is not possible to serve the concurrent writ out of the jurisdiction, see (*b*) below. The original writ may always be served within the jurisdiction if that becomes possible.

(b) Outside

Order 65, r 4, applies to a writ issued for service out of the jurisdiction (Ord 11, r 5(1)). As before the method of substituted service requested must be likely to bring the document to the defendant's attention. Note that substituted service may be ordered within the jurisdiction as well as outside (*Western Suburban* v *Rucklidge* [1905] 2 Ch 472).

In *Myerson* v *Martin* [1979] 1 WLR 1390, the Court of Appeal refused to allow substituted service of a writ issued at a time when the defendant was outside the jurisdiction in a case which did not fall within Ord 11, r 1. 'Where the defendant is abroad and the case is outside the court's jurisdiction under Ord 11, I do not think that the court should exercise its discretion under Ord 65, r 4 to order substituted service where the effect would be to add yet another cause of action to those listed in Ord 11' (per Eveleigh LJ at p 1396).

Chapter 8

Irregular Service

This chapter deals with the way in which a defendant who wishes to dispute that he has been validly served may do so. The introduction of the form of acknowledgement of service provided by RSC Ord 12 abolished the former distinction between the entry of ordinary and conditional appearances, and provided a new procedure for disputing jurisdiction.

1 Acknowledgement of service

A form of acknowledgement of service is served with every writ and originating summons. The mode of acknowledging service is provided by Ord 12, r 1 and explained by detailed notes in the *Supreme Court Practice*, paras 12/1/1–20. The forms themselves contain directions and notes for guidance on how to complete the acknowledgement.

The acknowledgement of service contains the defendant's address for service (Ord 12, r 3) and this is discussed in Chapter 3 (head 1).

By Ord 12, r 7, the acknowledgement by a defendant of service of a writ shall not be treated as a waiver by him of any irregularity in the writ or service thereof or in any order giving leave to serve the writ out of the jurisdiction or extending the validity of the writ for the purpose of service.

Order 12 applies to an originating summons in the same way as it applies to a writ (Ord 12, r 9).

2 Disputing jurisdiction

By Ord 12, r 8(1):

A defendant who wishes to dispute the jurisdiction of the court in the proceedings by reason of which any such irregularity as is mentioned in r 7 or on any other ground shall give notice of intention to defend the proceedings and shall, within the time limited for service of a defence, apply to the court for–

(a) an order setting aside the writ or service of the writ on him, or

(b) an order declaring that the writ has not been duly served on him or

(c) the discharge of any order giving leave to serve the writ on him out of the jurisdiction, or

(d) the discharge of any order extending the validity of the writ for the purpose of service, or

(e) the protection or release of any property of the defendant seized or threatened with seizure in the proceedings, or

(f) the discharge of any order made to prevent any dealing with any property of the defendant, or

(g) a declaration that in the circumstances of the case the court has no jurisdiction over the defendant in respect of the subject matter of the claim or the relief or remedy sought in the action, or

(h) such other relief as may be appropriate.

This chapter can only deal with questions of service (ie applications under r 8(1)(a)–(d)).

Note that the defendant may apply for more than one of the orders set out above at once.

It is not clear whether, within the time limited for service of a defence given by r 8(1) to 'apply to the court', the defendant must both issue *and* serve his application (*Carmel Exporters (Sales) Ltd v Sea-Land Services Inc* [1981] 1 WLR 1068). In that case Robert Goff J suggested that the Rule Committee should clarify or amend the words of the rule (at p 1079). To be on the safe side, the application should be served within the fourteen days. (Leave to appeal to the Court of Appeal was granted in *Carmel*).

A defendant wishing to make an application under r 8(1) should not serve a defence or do anything else to defend the merits of the action, lest this is regarded as a waiver of any irregularity. A defendant is, however, at liberty to apply to stay proceedings pending the outcome of proceedings in a foreign jurisdiction without falling foul of that principle: *Williams & Glyn's Bank plc v Astro Dinamico Cia Naviera SA* [1984] 1 WLR 438. Equally, a plaintiff must not enter judgment in default of defence while an application under r 8 is pending.

Even if judgment in default of notice of intention to defend has been entered, an application may be made provided the defendant obtains leave to give late notice of intention to defend and asks for judgment to be set aside.

By r 8(3), the application must be made

(*a*) in an Admiralty action in rem, by motion;

(*b*) in any other action in the Queen's Bench Division, by summons;

(*c*) in any other action, by summons or motion,

and the notice of motion or summons must state the grounds of the application. Failure to state the grounds fully is an irregularity under Ord 2, r 1, which may be corrected where the plaintiff has not been prejudiced. Leave to amend the application may be granted (*Carmel* case above).

By r 8(4), an application under r 8(1) must be supported by an affidavit verifying the facts on which the application is based, and a copy of the affidavit must be served with the notice of motion or summons. Again, where there is a failure to serve the affidavit in due time, this is an irregularity under Ord 2, r 1, which may be rectified where the plaintiff has not been prejudiced (*Carmel* case). The plaintiff may serve an affidavit in reply and contest the defendant's case (*Fowler* v *Bairstow* (1881) 20 Ch D 240).

The following are examples of cases where the writ or service may be challenged as being irregular under r 8(1):

(*a*) where it has been issued for service out of the jurisdiction without leave under Ord 6, r 7(1);

(*b*) where it has not been properly issued under Ord 11;

(*c*) where it contains no address of the defendant who lives out of the jurisdiction;

(*d*) where substituted service has been ordered on a defendant abroad who could not in law have been served personally;

(*e*) where service is more than 12 months after issue;

(*f*) where there is a non-trivial departure from the prescribed form;

(*g*) where service on a foreigner temporarily within the jurisdiction has been achieved as a result of his having been fraudulently enticed here for the purpose of effecting service (*Watkins* v *North American Land* (1904) 20 TLR 534).

Note that, prima facie, if a foreigner is temporarily within the jurisdiction, service on him is good.

The court may grant the application, or may remodel or limit an order for service to meet the justice of the case.

By r 8(5), the court, if it does not dispose of the matter in dispute, may give appropriate directions for its disposal, including directions for its trial as a preliminary issue.

If the court makes no order on, or dismisses, the application, the defendant's notice of intention to defend the action ceases to have effect and he should, if he wishes to defend on the merits, lodge a further acknowledgement of service (r 8(6)). He will then be treated as having submitted to the jurisdiction (r 8(7)).

Ord 12, r 8A provides for a defendant named in a writ which has *not* been served on him to serve a notice on the plaintiff requiring him within not less than 14 days thereafter either to serve the writ or discontinue the action. If the plaintiff fails to comply with the notice, the defendant can apply by summons (supported by an affidavit verifying the facts and stating that he intends to contest the proceedings), to have the action dismissed. The court may make such order as it thinks fit. If the plaintiff serves the writ after service of the defendant's notice, or pursuant to an order made by the court, the defendant must acknowledge service within the time limited for so doing.

Chapter 9

County Court Documents Generally

The rules for the service of documents in England and Wales are contained in CCR Ord 7. Part I of Ord 7 deals with the service of documents generally.

1 Methods of service

Where a document has to be served on a person under the rules and no other mode of service is prescribed by any Act or rule, Ord 7, r 1(1) provides that, if the person to be served is acting in person the document may be served:

(*a*) by delivering it to him personally, or

(*b*) by delivering it at, or sending it by first-class post to, his address for service (see below), or if he has no address for service:

    (i) by delivering the document at his residence or by sending it by first-class post to his last known residence; or

    (ii) in the case of a proprietor of a business, by delivering the document at his place of business or sending it by first-class post to his last known place of business.

If the person to be served is acting by a solicitor, (i) service may be made by delivering the document at, or sending it by first-class post to, the solicitor's address for service; or (ii) where the solicitor's address for service includes a numbered box at a document exchange, by leaving the document at that document exchange or at a document exchange which transmits documents daily to that document exchange.

Any document left at a document exchange shall, unless the

contrary is proved, be deemed to have been served on the second day after the day on which it is left (r 1(3)). Further, in determining (a) whether a document exchange transmits documents daily to another document exchange and (b) the second day after a document is left at a document exchange, any day on which the court office is closed is excluded (r 1(4)).

In Ord 7, 'first-class post' means first-class post which has been pre-paid or in respect of which prepayment is not required (r 1(2)).

The following document exchanges have been approved by the Lord Chancellor for service under this order: Britdoc Ltd of Hayes Wharf, Guildford, Surrey, Northern Document Exchange Ltd of 9a Middlesborough Wharf, Depot Road, Middlesborough, Cleveland, and at Bristol Commercial Rooms, Corn Street, Bristol.

'Address for service' is defined in Ord 1, r 3, as the address of a place at or to which any document may be delivered or sent for the party giving the address, being:

(*a*) in the case of a party in person, his place of residence or business or, if he has no such place within England or Wales, the address of a place within England or Wales at or to which documents for him may be delivered or sent,

(*b*) where the party is represented by a solicitor, the business address of the solicitor.

Particulars of claim, admission, defence and counterclaim in an action must each contain the address for service of the party serving the pleading (Ord 6, r 8; Ord 9 r 19).

Personal service is effected by leaving the document with the person to be served (Ord 7, r 2(*a*)). Reference should be made to Chapter 1 for decisions on what amounts to personal service (head 5).

By Ord 7, r 5, where a bailiff is prevented by the violence or threats of the person to be served, or any person acting in concert with him, from serving a document in accordance with Ord 7, it is sufficient service to leave the document as near as practicable to the person to be served.

By Ord 7, r 2(*b*), the document may be served by:

(*a*) a bailiff of the court or, if the person to be served attends at the office of the court, any other officer of the court; or

(*b*) a party to the proceedings or some other person acting as his agent (note the change in the rule from the old Ord 8, r 2(*b*)(ii) which required the person to be in the party's 'permanent and exclusive employ') or

(*c*) the solicitor of a party or a solicitor acting as an agent for such solicitor or some person employed by either solicitor to serve the document.

The person serving the document must not be under sixteen years of age.

Apart from an admiralty summons in rem which may be served on any day (Ord 40, r 5(5)), no process may be served or executed within England or Wales on a Sunday, Good Friday or Christmas Day except, in case of urgency, with the leave of the court.

Reference should be made to Chapter 1, head 3, for a discussion of certain places where service probably should not be attempted.

Any process to be served or executed by the bailiff of any court may be served or executed with a distance of not more than 500 yards beyond the boundary of the district of that court (Ord 7, r 4(1)), although any process to be served or executed by bailiff may, if the judge or registrar of the court from which it issues so directs, be served or executed within the district of any other court by the bailiff of the court from which the process issues (r 4(2)).

2 Proof of service

If the person who has effected service is an officer of the court, he must make, sign and file a certificate showing the date, place and mode of service and any conduct money paid or tendered to the person served (Ord 7, r 6(1)(a)). If he is not an officer of the court, he must file an affidavit of service (r 6(1)(b)). For form of affidavit, see Form 18 in Appendix 2.

A bailiff who has filed to effect service of any document to be served by bailiff must make, sign and file a certificate of non-service showing the reason why service has not been effected, and the proper officer of the bailiff's court shall send notice of non-service to the person at whose instance the document was issued (r 6(2)).

'Proper officer' is defined by Ord 1, r 3 as the registrar or, in relation to any act of a formal or administrative character which is not by statute the responsibility of the registrar, the chief clerk or any other officer of the court acting on his behalf in accordance with directions given by the Lord Chancellor.

3 Service in a foreign district

By Ord 7, r 7, where a document is to be served by bailiff in a foreign court, the proper officer sends the document and all necessary copies to the foreign court. On the filing of a certificate of service or non-service under Ord 7, r 6, the proper officer of the foreign court sends it to the home court with any copied of the document in his possession.

4 Substituted service

The use of substituted service is generally encountered in relation to documents which must be served personally, where problems arise in attempting to do so. Since summonses may be served by post (see Chapter 10), substituted service will only infrequently be needed there.

Order 7, r 8(1) provides that if it appears to the court that it is impracticable for any reason to serve a document in any manner prescribed by the rules for the service of that document, the court may, upon an affidavit showing grounds, make an order for substituted service giving leave for such steps to be taken as the court directs to bring the document to the notice of the person to be served.

See Chapter 7 as to what the affidavit should contain and what types of substituted service are ordered.

Where a document is to be served by bailiff, the proper officer of the bailiff's court must, if so requested, take such steps as may be necessary to provide evidence on which an order for substituted service may be made (Ord 7, r 8(2)).

5 Computation of time

Order 1, r 9 explains how a period of time fixed by the rules or by a judgment, order or direction for carrying out an act must be reckoned.

Rule 9 provides that where the act is required to be done:

(*a*) not less than a specified period before a specified date, the period starts immediately after the date 'on which the act is done and ends immediately before the specified date (r 9(2));

(*b*) within a specified period after or from a specified date, the period starts immediately after that date (r 9(3)).

Order 1, r 9(4) provides that where, apart from this paragraph, the period in question being a period of three days or less would include a day on which the court office is closed, that day shall be excluded.

By Ord 2, r 2, every court office must be open on every day of the year *except*:

(*a*) Saturdays and Sundays;

(*b*) the day before Good Friday from noon onwards and Good Friday;

(*c*) the Tuesday after the spring holiday (defined by r 2(2) as the bank holiday on the last Monday in May or any day appointed instead of that day under the Banking and Financial Dealings Act 1971, s 1(2));

(*d*) Christmas Eve or, if that day is a Saturday, 23 December, or, if that day is a Sunday or a Tuesday, 27 December;

(*e*) Christmas Day and, if that day is a Friday or Saturday, then 28 December;

(*f*) bank holidays (defined by r 2(2) as bank holidays in England and Wales under the Banking and Financial Dealings Act 1971); and

(*g*) such other days as the Lord Chancellor may by general or special order direct.

Where the time fixed for doing an act (under r 9) in the court office expires on a day on which the office is closed, and for that reason the act cannot be done on that day, the act shall be in time if done on the next day on which the office is open (Ord 1, r 9(5)).

Chapter 10

County Court Summonses

The rules for the service of default and fixed date summonses (together called 'summonses' (CCR Ord 7, r 9)) are contained in CCR Ord 7, Pt II.

Unlike the service of High Court process, service of proceedings in the county court is usually carried out by the registrar and his staff, rather than the plaintiff or his solicitor; though the latter are given the option of serving summonses personally. The plaintiff or his solicitor chooses the mode of service when commencing proceedings under CCR Ord 3 (as to which, see Chapter 11).

1 Methods of service

Subject to the provisions of any Act or rule a summons must be effected by one of two ways:

(a) Unless the plaintiff or his solicitor requests otherwise, an officer of the court sends the summons by first class post to the defendant at the address stated in the request for summons;

(b) If the plaintiff or his solicitor so requests, the plaintiff delivers the summons to the defendant personally (Ord 7, r 10(1) and (2)).

Thus, in the first instance, personal service may only be effected by the plaintiff, and not by the court bailiff.

If the summons is to be served personally by the plaintiff, the proper officer will, when the plaintiff commences the proceedings under Ord 3, r 3, deliver to him for service under Ord 7 the summons and all necessary copies, with any documents required to be annexed thereto (Ord 3, r 3(2)(d)(ii)).

Where a summons has been sent by post under r 10(1) to the address stated in the request for the summons and has been returned to the court office undelivered, notice of non-service shall be sent pursuant to r 6(2) together with a notice informing the plaintiff that he may request bailiff service at that address. If the plaintiff then requests bailiff service, the bailiff must serve the summons:

(a) by inserting the summons, enclosed in an envelope addressed to the defendant, through the letter box at the address stated in the request for the summons, or

(b) by delivering the summons to some person, apparently not less than 16 years old, at the address stated in the request for the summons, or

(c) by delivering it to the defendant personally (r 10(4)).

2 Time for service

Initially, the time within which a summons may be served is limited to twelve months from its date of issue (Ord 7, r 20(1)).

However, by Ord 7, r 20(2), the court may extend the period for service of a summons from time to time for such period, not exceeding twelve months at any one time, beginning with the day next following that on which it would otherwise expire, as the court may specify, if an application for extension is made before that day or such later day (if any) as the court may allow.

In addition to the above, a fixed date summons must ordinarily be served not less than twenty-one days before the return day (Ord 7, r 10(5)). However, if the plaintiff satisfies the registrar by affidavit that the defendant is on the point of moving from the address stated in the request for the summons, service may be effected at any time before the return day. This provision is without prejudice to the general power of the court to abridge time limits under Ord 13, r 4 (see Chapter 12, head 1).

Further, where a fixed date summons has been duly served, but it appears to have come to the defendant's knowledge less than twenty-one days before the return day, the court may, without prejudice to its powers under Ord 7, r 10(5), or Ord 13, r 4, allow the action to proceed whether or not the defendant appears on the return day; or adjourn the hearing or, as the case may be, the pre-trial review (CCR Ord 7, r 16).

Where a summons is served by post under Ord 7, r 10(1), the date of service is deemed (unless the contrary is shown) to be the seventh day after the date when the summons was sent (Ord 7, r 10(3)).

3 Proof of service

For proof of service, see Chapter 9, head 2.

Where a summons has not been served in accordance with Ord 7, r 10 but the defendant delivers to the court office a defence, admission or counterclaim, the summons is deemed, unless the contrary is shown, to have been duly served on him on the date on which the defence, admission or counterclaim was so delivered (Ord 7, r 12).

4 Notice of service or non-service

Where a default summons has been served by a bailiff or other officer of a county court, the proper officer of that court must send notice of service to the plaintiff (Ord 7, r 21). For form of notice, see Appendix 2, Form 19. Otherwise, see Chapter 9, head 2.

5 Acceptance of service by solicitor

Where a defendant's solicitor gives a certificate that he accepts service of the summons on behalf of that defendant and stating an address for service, the summons is deemed to have been duly served on that defendant on the date on which the certificate was made (Ord 7, r 11).

6 Amendment

Order 7, r 17(1) provides that, subject to r 17(2)–(4), a summons which has not been served may be amended on the plaintiff filing an amended request for the issue of the summons.

An amendment may be made under r 17(1) notwithstanding that it consists of the addition or substitution of a defendant, but in that case Ord 15, r 2(3), applies to the amendment as it applies to an amendment made under Ord 15, r 1. See Summonses for recovery of land, (head 9 below).

If the bailiff by whom a summons is to be served ascertains before notice of non-service has been sent that the defendant has removed from the address stated on the summons to a new address within the district of the court, it is his duty to serve the summons without amendment and to state the new address in his certificate of service (Ord 7, r 17(3)).

Where the defendant's address stated in the request for the issue of the summons was within the district of the court and at the time of the entry of the plaint the defendant was not residing or carrying on business within the district, an amendment of the address is allowed only on the plaintiff filing a fresh request for the issue of the summons showing that the court had jurisdiction under Ord 4, r 2, to entertain the action (Ord 7, r 17(4)).

Where by an order under Ord 15, r 1(1), a person is added or substituted as a defendant, the amended originating process must, unless the court otherwise directs, be served on him in accordance with the rules applicable to the service of the originating process (Ord 15, r 1(6)). The same applies, mutatis mutandis, to a defendant to a counterclaim.

7 Doubtful service

If it appears from the certificate of service of a summons that it has been delivered to a person under Ord 7, r 10(4)(*b*), but it is doubtful whether the court will be satisfied that the summons has come to the defendant's knowledge in sufficient time (defined below), the proper officer of the court for the district in which the summons is to be served must give to the plaintiff notice of doubtful service (Ord 7, r 18(1)).

Where such a notice has been given and the defendant does not deliver a defence, admission or counterclaim or, in the case of a fixed date summons, does not appear on the return day, the plaintiff may be required to satisfy the court that the summons has come to the defendant's knowledge in sufficient time (Ord 7, r 18(2)).

'Sufficient time' is defined by r 18(3) as:

(*a*) in the case of a default summons, sufficient time for the defendant to deliver a defence, admission or counterclaim within fourteen days after delivery of the summons under Ord 7, r 10(4)(*b*) (See Chapter 9, head 5, for the computation of time); and

(*b*) in the case of a fixed date summons, sufficient time for him to attend on the return day.

8 Successive summonses

Order 7, r 19(1) provides that, where a fixed date summons has not been served on every defendant, successive summonses may from time to time be issued without entering a new plaint, on the plaintiff filing an amended request on each occasion when a successive summons is to be issued.

Where a fixed date summons has not been served by reason of a defendant having, after entry of the plaint, moved out of the district in which the summons was required to be served, successive summonses may from time to time be issued for service in any district to which he has moved (r 19(2)).

A successive summons must bear the same date and number as the original summons; and be a continuance of the original summons; and be served in accordance with Ord 7, r 10 (r 19(2)).

9 Summonses for recovery of land

Where a summons for the recovery of land is to be served by bailiff, and the court's opinion is that it is impracticable to serve it in accordance with the ordinary rules under Ord 7, it may be served under Ord 7, r 15 (r 15(1)).

By r 15(2), the summons may be served on any person on the premises who is the husband or wife of the defendant or on any person who has or appears to have the authority of the defendant to reside or carry on business in the premises or to manage them on behalf of the defendant or to receive any rents or profits of the premises or to pay any outgoings in respect of the premises; or to safeguard or deal with the premises or with the furniture or other goods on the premises. Service on any such person is effected in the manner required by the rules with respect to a fixed date summons (ibid).

Rule 15(2) applies to a man and woman who are living with each other in the same household as husband and wife as it applies to spouses (Ord 7, r 15(3)).

Where premises are vacant, or occupied only by virtue of the presence of furniture or other goods, the summons may be served by affixing it to some conspicuous part of the premises (Ord 7, r 15(4)).

Unless the court otherwise orders, service of a summons under r 15 is good service on the defendant, but if a claim for the recovery of money is joined with the claim for recovery of land, the court must order the summons to be marked 'not served' with respect to the money claim unless in special circumstances the court thinks it just to hear and determine both claims (Ord 7, r 15(5)).

A summons in a rent action with a copy of the particulars of claim attached must be served on the defendant in accordance with Ord 7, r 1 not less than seven clear days before the return day (Ord 24, r 10).

10 Specific defendants

(a) The Crown

By Ord 42, r 7(3) a document is served on the Crown either:

(a) by leaving it at the office of the person to be served in accordance with the Crown Proceedings Act 1947, s 18 (see Chapter 5, head 1), or any agent whom he has nominated for the purpose, but in either case with a member of the staff of that person or agent; or

(b) by posting it in a prepaid envelope addressed to the person to be served in accordance with s 18 or to any such agent.

Personal service of any document in civil proceedings by or against the Crown is *never* required (Ord 42, r 7(2)).

(b) Members of the armed forces

The *Memorandum on Service of Legal Process on Members of Her Majesty's Forces*, issued by the Lord Chancellor's Office on 26 July 1979 (see Chapter 5, head 2), has effect in respect of county court process.

(c) Partners

Service of summonses on partners is governed by Ord 7, r 13. Rule 13(1) provides that, subject to r 13(2)–(4), where partners are sued in the name of their firm, service of a summons is good service on all the partners, whether any of them is out of England and Wales or not, if it is delivered to a partner personally, or served by an officer of the court sending it by first class post to the firm at the address stated in the request for the summons. Where, however, the partnership has to the knowledge of the plaintiff been dissolved before the commencement of the action, the summons shall be served upon every person within England and Wales sought to be made liable (r 13(2)).

The rules relating to service by post (r 10(2) and (3), (see head 1 supra) apply to service by post on a firm (r 13(3)). Rule 10(4) also applies to service on a firm with modifications; the alternative methods of bailiff service are:

(a) as before,

(b) by delivering the summons at the principal place of the partnership business within the district within which the summons is to be served to any person having, or appearing to have, at the time of service, the control or management of the business there, or (*c*) by delivering the summons to a partner personally (r 13(4)).

Rule 14(2) provides that service of a summons on a company registered in England and Wales may be effected by serving it at the registered office or at any place of business of the company which has some real connection with the cause or matter in issue. This rule is, therefore, less stringent than s 725 of the Companies Act 1985.

(d) Corporate bodies

Order 7, r 14(1) provides that service of a summons on a body corporate may, in cases for which provision is not otherwise made by an enactment, be effected by serving it on the mayor, chairman or president of the body or the town clerk, clerk, secretary, treasurer or other similar officer thereof.

However, where such service is other than at the registered office, and, after judgment has been entered or given or an order has been made, it appears to the court that the summons did not come to the knowledge of an appropriate person within the company in due time, the court may, upon application or of its own motion, set aside the judgment or order and may give such directions as it thinks fit (r 14(3)).

As to companies and friendly societies, where service is governed by a statutory provision (eg a limited company), see Chapter 5.

(e) Persons under disability

Service on persons under a disability is governed by CCR Ord 10, r 4.

Where the defendant is a minor and not also a mental patient, a summons must be served on one of his parents or his guardian or, if he has no parent or guardian, on the person with whom he resides or in whose care he is (r 4(1)(*a*)).

Where the defendant is a mental patient, a summons must be served on the person (if any) who is authorised under the Mental Health Act 1983, Pt VII, to conduct in the name of the mental patient or on his behalf the proceedings in connection with which the summons is to be served or, if there is no person so authorised, on the person with whom he resides or in whose care he is (r 4(1)(*b*)).

In both cases the summons is served on the recipient in the normal way for that type of summons (r 4(1)), and, notwithstanding r 4(1)(*a*) or (*b*), the court may order that any summons which has been, or is to be, served on the person under disability or on a person other than a person mentioned above will be deemed to be duly served on the person under disability (r 4(2)).

Chapter 11

Other County Court Process

This chapter deals with the procedure for service of originating applications, petitions and summonses in Admiralty actions.

The general rules as to service of an originating application are contained in CCR Ord 3, r 4, discussed below. In the case of originating applications under certain Acts these rules are modified in the ways set out thereafter.

1 Originating applications generally

By Ord 3, r 4(2), an originating application must state, inter alia, the names and addresses of the persons (if any) intended to be served (called 'respondents') or that no person is intended to be served, and the applicant's address for service (see Chapter 9, head 1).

On the filing of the application, the proper officer enters the originating application in the records of the court and fixes a return day (being a day fixed for the hearing of the application, or a pretrial review). He then prepares, inter alia, a notice to each respondent of the return day and annexes to each notice a copy of the application.

If the originating application is to be served otherwise than by an officer of the court, the proper officer sends to the plaintiff, inter alia, the application and all necessary copies, with any documents required to be annexed thereto, for service in accordance with Ord 7 (r 4(6)).

The answer to an originating application (where one is required by the rules) must be filed within fourteen days after the date of service of the application on the respondent, and must be accompanied by as many copies as there are parties to the proceedings (Ord 9, r 18(3)). The answer must state the respondent's address for service (Ord 9, r 19).

On receipt of the answer and copies, the proper officer must send a copy to the applicant and to every other party to the proceedings.

2 Summary proceedings for recovery of land

In the summary proceedings for the recovery of land under Ord 24, where any person in occupation of the land is named in the originating application, r 3(1) provides that it must be served on him:

(a) by delivering to him personally a copy of the originating application, together with the notice of the return day required by Ord 3, r 4(4)(b), and a copy of the affidavit in support; or

(b) by an officer of the court leaving the documents mentioned above or sending them to him, at the premises; or

(c) in accordance with Ord 7, r 11 (see Chapter 10, head 5), as applied in originating applications by Ord 3, r 4(6); or

(d) in such other manner as the court may direct.

The originating application must, in addition to being served on the named respondents (if any) as above, be served, unless the court otherwise directs, by (i) affixing a copy of each of the documents mentioned in (a) above to the main door or other conspicuous part of the premises, and, if practicable, inserting through the letter box at the premises a copy of those documents enclosed in a sealed envelope addressed to 'the occupiers' or (ii) placing stakes in the ground at conspicuous parts of the occupied land, to each of which shall be affixed a sealed transparent envelope addressed to 'the occupier' and containing a copy of each of the documents mentioned above (rule 3(2)).

By Ord 24, r 5(1), except in case of urgency and by leave of the court, the day fixed for the hearing of the originating applications in the case of residential premises must not be less than five days after the day of service; in the case of other land, two days.

3 Proceedings under the Rent Act 1977

Applications to the county court under the Rent Act 1977 made under the Rent (County Court Proceedings) Rules 1970 are by originating application: the documents required by Ord 3, r 4, to be served on each respondent must be served not less than ten or, in the case of an application for leave to distrain, not less than four clear days before the hearing day (1970 Rules, r 3(3)).

By r 3(4), service may be effected in accordance with the old Ord 8, r 39 (now Ord 7, r 1) by any person authorised by the old Ord 8, r 2 (now Ord 7, r 2) to effect personal service of a document and by any officer of the court where service is to be effected by post. Service of an application for leave to distrain may also be effected by any person regularly authorised by or on behalf of the applicant to collect the rent of the premises in question.

The Rent Act (County Court Proceedings for Possession) Rules 1981 provide an originating application procedure for possession claims under Cases 11–20 in the Rent Act 1977, Sched 15, in the circumstances set out in r 2.

Service of the originating application (if the form prescribed in the Appendices to the Rules) is as in the CCR. By r 5(1), where possession is claimed under Cases 11, 12 or 20, each respondent must be served at least seven clear days before the return day and in any other Case, at least fourteen clear days before the return day. Order 7, r 15 (see Chapter 10, head 9) applies to the application with such modifications as may be necessary, as if it were a summons in an action for the recovery of land (r 5(2)).

The affidavit in support under r 4 must be served on the respondent together with the documents mentioned in Ord 3, r 4.

4 Proceedings under the Landlord and Tenants Acts 1927, 1954, 1985 and 1987

Except for an application under the Landlord and Tenant Act 1954, s 13, for the recovery of possession, which is brought by action, all proceedings under the Landlord and Tenant Acts 1927, 1954, 1985 and 1987 are commenced by originating application, and the respondent must file an answer (Ord 43, r 2(1)).

An application for a new tenancy under the 1954 Act, s 24, must be made within two months of its date of issue, since Ord 7, r 20, applies with the substitution of two months for twelve months (Ord 43, r 6(3) and see Chapter 10, head 2). There is power under Ord 13, r 4 (see Chapter 12, head 1), to extend this time limit in a proper case (*Lewis* v *Wolking Properties* [1978] 1 WLR 403).

The return day is, generally, a day fixed for the pre-trial review of the proceedings (Ord 43, r 2(2)), where it is convenient to decide whether any other persons ought to be joined in the proceedings and given notice of them.

A copy of any order made on an application under Pt II of the 1954 Act is sent by the proper officer to every party to the proceedings (Ord 43, r 10).

5 Adoption applications

Any notice or information required to be given under the Adoption Act 1976 may be given by post (s 69). The Adoption Rules 1984 deal with the procedure for adoption and freeing applications in the county court. By r 50, unless otherwise directed, any document under the rules may be served:

(a) on a corporation or body of persons, by delivering it at, or sending it by post to, the registered or principal office of the corporation or body;

(b) on any other person, by delivering it to him, or by sending it by post to him at his usual or last known address.

The server must make, sign and file a certificate showing the date, place and mode of service, or in the case of failure, a certificate of non-service showing the reason why service has not been effected (r 50(2)).

The originating application is in Form 1 (freeing application) or Form 6 (adoption application). This is filed in the court office. The proper officer then appoints a reporting officer/guardian ad litem as appropriate and send him a copy of the application and any documents attached thereto. As soon as practicable, the proper officer lists the case for hearing and serves notice of the hearing on all the parties, the reporting officer and the guardian (if appointed) (rr 9 and 21). Only the guardian, reporting officer and local authority (where the 1976 Act, s 22 applies) shall be served with the originating application.

Rule 52 deals with the service by the proper officer of notice of the making or refusal of an order under the Adoption Act.

6 Petitions

Where by any Act or rule proceedings in a county court are required to be by petition, Ord 3, r 4, applies to the petition as it applies to an originating application but with the substitution of 'petitioner' for 'applicant' and 'petition' for 'originating application' or 'application', wherever those expressions occur (Ord 3, r 5). This rule does not apply to divorce petitions, but to those Acts which provide that the process to be used should be a petition, eg, certain proceedings under the Companies Act 1985.

7 Admiralty actions

The summons in an action in personam may be served in any manner prescribed by the CCR for the service of a default summons (see Chapter 10) (Ord 40, r 6(1)).

Where an action in personam is commenced under Ord 40, r 2(2)(*a*), in the court for the district in which an agent resides or carries on business, the summons must be served on the agent (Ord 40, r 6(2)).

The summons in an action in rem may be served on a solicitor under Ord 7, r 11 (see Chapter 10, head 5) (Ord 40, r 5(6)). Subject to that exception, the summons *and* any warrant of arrest issued in an action in rem must be served on the property against which it is issued except where the property is freight, in which case they must be served on the cargo in respect of which the freight is payable or on the ship in which the cargo was carried (Ord 40, r 5(1)).

The mode of service depends on whether or not the summons was issued against freight or cargo. If the summons/warrant was issued against freight or cargo, and the cargo has been landed or transhipped, service is effected by leaving the summons or duplicate warrant on the cargo, or, if the cargo is in the custody of a person who will not permit access to it, by leaving the summons or duplicate warrant with that person (Ord 40, r 5(3)). Otherwise, service is effected by affixing the summons or duplicate warrant on any mast of the ship or on the outside of any part of the ship's superstructure, or by delivering the summons or duplicate of the warrant to the person who is, at the time of service, apparently in charge of the ship or other property (Ord 40, r 5(2)).

Service of the summons may be effected by any of the persons mentioned in Ord 7, r 2(*b*) (see Chapter 9, head 1) (Ord 40, r 5(4)).

The summons/warrant of arrest may be served on any day, *including* Sunday, Good Friday and Christmas Day (Ord 40, r 5(5)).

Chapter 12

Other County Court Documents

1 Applications in the course of proceedings

Except as otherwise provided, CCR Ord 13, r 1 has effect in relation to an application made at any stage in the course of an action or matter (Ord 13, r 1(1)).

Where the application is made on notice, it must be filed and served on the opposite party not less than two days before the hearing of the application (Ord 13, r 1(2)), and see Chapter 9, head 5, on the computation of time.

Where the application is made ex parte, notice of the application must be filed a reasonable time before the application is heard, unless the court otherwise directs (Ord 13, r 1(3)).

Extension of time is governed by Ord 13, r 4(1), which states that, except as otherwise provided, the period within which a person is required or authorised by the CCR or by any judgment, order or direction to do any act in any proceedings may be extended or abridged by consent of all the parties or by the court on the application of any party. Any such period may be extended by the court even if an application for extension is not made until after the expiration of the period (r 4(2)).

2 Witness summonses

A witness summons shall not be issued less than seven days before the date upon which attendance is required, unless the judge or registrar otherwise directs. It must be served on the witness not less than four days before the hearing, again unless the court otherwise directs: Ord 20, r 12(4)(a). Subject to r 12(5), a witness summons must be served personally.

Rule 12(5), provides that where the applicant or his solicitor gives a certificate for postal service, the summons must, unless the registrar otherwise directs, be served on the witness by an officer of the court sending it to him by first-class post at the address stated in the request for the summons. Unless the contrary is shown, the date of service is deemed to be the seventh day after the date on which the summons was sent to the witness.

At the time of service the witness must be paid or tendered £8.50 (£6 for a police officer) plus reasonable travelling expenses to and from court (r 12(7)).

3 Notices to admit facts

A notice to admit facts specified in a notice under Ord 20, r 2(1), must be served not later than fourteen days before the trial or hearing. If the party served with the notice does not deliver a written admission of the facts within seven days after service of the notice on him, he will normally have to pay the costs of proving the facts (r 2(2)).

4 Notices to admit or produce documents

A party may, not later than fourteen days before the trial or hearing of an action or matter, serve on another party a notice requiring him to admit the authenticity of a document which he wishes to adduce in evidence (Ord 20, r 3(1)).

If the recipient of the notice wishes to challenge the document's authenticity, he must, within seven days after service of the notice, serve on the party by whom it was given a notice that he does not admit the authenticity of the document and requires it to be proved at the trial. In that case, he will normally be required to pay the costs of proving it (r 3(2)). If he does not serve a counter-notice, he will normally be deemed to have admitted the document (r 3(3)).

One party may serve on another a notice requiring him to produce the document specified in the notice at the trial/hearing (r 3(4)).

5 Attachment of earnings

Notice of an application for an attachment of earnings order made under Ord 27, r 4, together with a form of reply, must be served on the debtor in the same manner as a fixed date summons (for which see Chapter 10) (Ord 27, r 5(1)).

By r 5(2), the debtor must, within eight days after service on him of those documents, file a reply in the form provided, and the instruction to that effect in the notice to the debtor constitutes a requirement imposed by virtue of the Attachment of Earnings Act 1971, s 14(4). However, no proceedings may be taken for an offence alleged to have been committed under the 1971 Act, s 23(2)(c) or (f) in relation to the requirement unless the documents specified have been served on the debtor personally or the court is satisfied that they came to him knowledge in sufficient time for him to comply with the requirement (ibid).

When the proper officer receives a reply, he sends a copy to the applicant (r 5(3)).

An attachment of earnings order and any order varying or discharging such an order must be served on the debtor and on the person to whom the order is directed (Ord 27, r 10(2)).

Ord 7, r 1 (see Chapter 9, head 1) applies to such service with the following modifications:

(a) where the person to be served is acting by a solicitor, service may, if the court thinks fit, be effected on the person as if he *were* acting in person (Ord 22, r 1(5), as applied by Ord 27, r 10(2));

(b) where the order is directed to a corporation which has requested the court that any communication relating to the debtor or to the class of persons to whom he belongs should be directed to the corporation at a particular address, service may, if the registrar thinks fit, be effected on the corporation at that address (Ord 27, r 10(2)).

Where the order is made to enforce a judgment/order of the High Court or a magistrates' court, the proper officer sends the order (or discharge) there too (Ord 27, r 10(3)).

6 Applications for summary judgment

An application for summary judgment under Ord 9, r 14, is served pursuant to r 14(3). Notice of the application, together with a copy of the affidavit in support and of any exhibits referred to therein, must be served on the defendant not less than seven days before the day fixed for the hearing of the application. See Chapter 9, head 5, for the computation of time.

7 Appeals to a county court

Order 3, r 6 sets out the procedure to be carried out on an appeal to a county court from a decision etc of a tribunal, where such an appeal lies under a statute.

After the appellant had filed the documents required by Ord 3, r 6(2) and (3), and the proper officer has acted in accordance with r 6(4), the request for the entry of the appeal is served in accordance with Ord 7 as if the notice of the day of hearing were a fixed date summons, and Ord 3, r 3(2)(*d*)(ii)(see Chapter 10, head 1) applies.

8 Garnishee proceedings

An order under Ord 30, r 1, directing a garnishee to show cause is drawn up by the proper officer with sufficient copies for service under Ord 30, r 3 (r 3(1)).

By Ord 30, r 3(2), unless otherwise directed, at least fifteen days before the return day a copy of the order must be served on the garnishee in the same manner as a fixed date summons (see Chapter 10). At least seven days after such service and at least seven days before the return day a copy must similarly be served on the judgment debtor in accordance with Ord 7, r 1 (see Chapter 9, head 1) (ibid). As from such service on the garnishee the order binds in his hands any debt due or accruing due from the garnishee to the judgment debtor, or so much thereof as is sufficient to satisfy the judgment or order obtained by the judgment creditor against the judgment debtor, and the costs entered on the order to show cause (ibid).

Note that there is no longer a requirement for personal service.

9 Interpleader proceedings

In interpleader proceedings under execution, once interpleader summonses have been issued by the registrar under CCR Ord 33, r 4, and a hearing date has been fixed by the proper officer, the summons must be served on the execution creditor and the claimant in the same manner as a fixed date summons (for which, see Chapter 10) (Ord 33, r 4(3)).

Without prejudice to Ord 13, r 4 (power to extend time: see head 1 above), service must be effected not less than fourteen days before the return day (see Chapter 9, head 5, for the computation of time).

In proceedings other than under execution, the applicant (ie a person under a liability etc to two or more claimants (Ord 33, r 6)) files an affidavit in the court office. Where the applicant is a defendant in a pending action, he must file the affidavit (and as many copies as there are claimants) within fourteen days after service on him of the summons in the action (Ord 33, r 7(*a*)).

After a return day has been fixed, notice of the application (which is prepared by the proper officer) must be given to the claimant(s), the applicant and the plaintiff in the action.

The notice to the claimant(s) must be served on him, together with the affidavit (under r 6(3)) and the summons and particulars of claim in the action, not less than twenty-one days before the return day in the same manner as a fixed date summons (see Chapter 10) (Ord 33, r 7(*d*)).

The proper officer sends notice to the applicant and plaintiff (r 7(*e*)).

Where the applicant is not a defendant in a pending action, the summons plus copy affidavit alone are served on each claimant in the same way as the notice above (Ord 33, r 8(*c*)).

10 Committal orders

Where a judgment or order under Ord 29, r 1(1), may be enforced by a committal order against a person, Ord 29, r 1(2) provides that, subject to r 1(6) and (7) it cannot be enforced unless:

(*a*) a copy of the judgment or order has been served *personally* on the person required to do or abstain from doing the act in question and also, where that person is a body corporate, on the director or other officer of the body against whom a committal order is sought; and

(*b*) in the case of a judgment or order requiring a person to do an act, the copy has been so served before the expiration of the time within which he was required to do the act and was accompanied by a copy of any order, made between the date of the judgment or order and the date of service, fixing that time.

The order of judgment, if in the nature of an injunction, or otherwise at the judgment creditor's request, is drawn up and issued by the proper officer, indorsed with or incorporating a notice as to the consequences of disobedience (a penal notice), for service under r 1(2) (r1 (3)).

If the person served with the judgment/order fails to obey it, the proper officer shall, at the judgment creditor's request, issue a notice calling on that person to show cause why a committal order should not be made against him, and subject to r 1(7) (below) the notice must be served *personally* (r 1(4)).

If a committal order is made, the order is for the issue of a warrant of committal and a copy of the order must be served on the person to be committed either before or at the time of the execution of the warrant, unless the judge otherwise orders (r 1(5)).

Service under r 1(2) is not a prerequisite where the judge is satisfied that, pending such service, the person against whom it is sought to enforce the judgment or order has had notice thereof either:

(a) by being present when the judgment or order was given or made, or

(b) by being notified of the terms of the judgment or order whether by telephone, telegram or otherwise (r 1(6)).

Without prejudice to its powers under Ord 7, r 8 (ie to order substituted service: see Chapter 9, head 4), the court may dispense with service of a copy of a judgment or order under r 1(2) or a notice to show cause under r 1(4), if the court thinks it just to do so (r 1(7)). (The specific mention of substituted service in this paragraph enacts the decision in *Worboys* v *Worboys* [1953] P 192).

11 Judgments and orders

By Ord 22, r 1(1), subject to the provisions of the Rules with respect to particular judgments and orders, every judgment or final order and every order for directions made under Ord 13, r 2, or Ord 17, r 1, must, unless the court otherwise directs, be drawn up and served by the proper officer on the party against whom it was given or made.

Service must be effected in accordance with Ord 7, r 1 (see Chapter 9, head 1), and it is not necessary for the party in whose favour the judgment or order was made to prove that it reached the party to be served (r 1(2)).

Where the party to be served is acting by a solicitor, service may, if the court thinks fit, be effected on the party as if he were acting in person (r 1(5)).

Where judgment is entered in a default action under Ord 9, r 6(1), for payment forthwith, it is not necessary to draw up and serve the judgment unless:

(a) the judgment is for payment to the plaintiff or his solicitor;

(b) the plaintiff has abandoned part of his claim otherwise than by amending his particulars of claim and serving a copy on the defendant;

(c) the judgment is an interlocutory judgment for damages to be assessed; or

(d) an application is to be made under Ord 35, r 3 (ie under s 12 of the Civil Jurisdiction and Judgments Act 1982).

A judgment given for the plaintiff in an action for principal money or interest secured by a mortgage or charge, and any order made on an appeal to a county court, is served on every party to the proceedings (Ord 22, r 1(4)).

12 Equity proceedings

Where in an action or matter for the administration of the estate of a deceased person, or the execution of a trust, or the sale of any property, the court gives a judgment or makes an order which affects the rights or interests of persons who are not parties to the action or matter, or directs any account to be taken or inquiry made, it may direct notice of the judgment or order to be served on any person interested in the estate or under the trust or in the property, as the case may be (Ord 23, r 1(1)).

The notice is drawn up by the proper officer (r 1(2)) and served in the same manner as a fixed date summons (see Chapter 10), unless the court feels that it is impracticable to serve a person, in which case service on him may be dispensed with (r 1(3)).

The order is still binding, even where service has been dispensed with, unless the judgment was obtained by fraud or material non-disclosure (r 1(4)). A person served may attend the proceedings, or apply to the judge or registrar (depending on who gave the judgment) within one month after service to discharge, vary or add to the judgment or order (r 1(5)).

13 Judgment summonses

By Ord 28, r 2(1), subject to r 2(2), a judgment summons must be served *personally* on every debtor against whom it is issued. See Chapter 9 for personal service.

Where the judgment creditor or his solicitor gives a certificate for postal service in respect of a debtor residing or carrying on business within the district of the court, the judgment summons must, unless the registrar otherwise directs, be served on that debtor by an officer of the court sending it to him by first-class post at the address stated in the request for the judgment summons and, unless the contrary is shown, the date of service is deemed to be the seventh day after the date on which the judgment summons was sent to the debtor (r 2(2)).

Where it is served by post, no order of commitment may be made against the debtor unless he appears at the hearing, or the judge is satisfied that the summons came to his knowledge in sufficient time for him to appear at the hearing (r 2(3)).

Where a judgment summons is served personally, there may, if the judgment creditor wishes, be paid to the debtor at the time of service a sum reasonably sufficient to cover his expenses in travelling to and from the court (r 2(4)).

A judgment summons must be served not less than fourteen days before the hearing date (r 3(1)) (see Chapter 9, head 5, for the computation of time).

When a judgment summons which has been sent by post is returned to the court office undelivered, a notice of non-service under Ord 7, r 6(2) (see Chapter 9, head 4) must be sent.

Order 7, rr 19 and 20 (see Chapter 10) apply, mutatis mutandis, to a judgment summons as they apply to a fixed date summons (Ord 28, r 3(3)).

14 Charging orders

A copy of a charging order nisi made under Ord 31, r 1(4), must be sent by the proper officer to the judgment creditor and, where funds in court are to be charged, must be served by the proper officer on the Accountant-General at the Court funds Office (r 1(5)). Copies of the order and affidavit in support must be served by the proper officer on the debtor and on such of the debtor's other creditors, and, where a trust is involved, on such trustees and beneficiaries as the registrar may direct (r 1(6)).

Where an interest in securities not in court is to be charged, copies of the order nisi must be served by the proper officer on the person or body required to be served in like circumstances by RSC Ord 50, r 2(1)(b) (see Chapter 3, head 8) (r 1(7)).

The documents to be served under Ord 31, r 1, must be served in accordance with Ord 7, r 1 (see Chapter 9, head 1), not less than seven days before the day fixed for the further consideration of the matter (see Chapter 9, head 5 for the computation of time) (r 1(8)).

If an order absolute is made, Ord 3, r 2, provides that a copy must be served by the proper officer in accordance with Ord 7, r 1, on each of the following:

(*a*) the debtor;

(*b*) the applicant for the order;

(*c*) where funds in court are charged, the Accountant-General at the Court Funds Office; and

(*d*) unless otherwise directed, any person or body on whom a copy of the order nisi was served pursuant to r 1(7), in which case the copy must contain a stop notice (Ord 31, r 2(2) and (3)).

15 Affidavits

Where a party desires to use at the hearing of an action or matter an affidavit which is not rendered admissible by Ord 20, r 5 (evidence in chambers), and in respect of which no order has been made under Ord 20, r 6, he may, not less than fourteen days before the hearing, give notice of his desire, accompanied by a copy of the affidavit, to the party against whom it is to be used. Unless the latter party, not less than seven days after receipt of the notice, gives notice to the other party that he objects to the use of the affidavit, he is taken to have consented to its use and accordingly the affidavit may be used at the hearing (Ord 20, r 7(1)).

No such notice is needed normally where the defendant in a fixed date action has not delivered a defence within the time limited by Ord 9, r 2, or the defendant in a default or fixed date action does not appear on a pre-trial review of the action (r 7(2)).

16 Amended pleadings

Whereas pleadings are filed in the court office, and then sent out to the other party by the court, where a pleading is amended without order under Ord 15, r 2(1), the amended pleading must be filed *and* served on the other party by the party amending (r 2(1)).

Chapter 13

Matrimonial Proceedings

The procedure governing service of documents in matrimonial proceedings is governed by the Matrimonial Causes Act 1973 and the Matrimonial Causes Rules 1977 (SI 1977 No 344).

1 Methods of service

MCR, rr 118 and 119 deal with the service of documents required by the rules to be sent to any person.

Where the person is acting by a solicitor, service is to be effected (subject to any other direction or order):

    (*a*) by sending the document by first-class post to the solicitor's address for service; or

    (*b*) where that address includes a numbered box at a document exchange, by leaving the document at that document exchange or at a document exchange with transmits documents daily to that document exchange (r 118(1)). Unless the contrary is proved, the document is deemed to be served on the second day after the day on which it is left at the document exchange (r 118(2)); or

    (*c*) where no other mode is prescribed, directed or ordered, service may additionally be effected by leaving the document at the solicitor's address (r 118(3)).

Where the individual is acting in person, service is effected by sending the document by first-class post to the address for service given by him or, if he has not given an address for service, to his last known address (r 119(1)). Where no other mode of service is prescribed, directed or ordered, service may additionally be effected by delivering the document to him or by leaving it at the address mentioned above (r 119(2)). These rules are subject to r 119(3), which permits the registrar to dispense with service if it appears to be impracticable to deliver the document to the person and that, if it were left at the address mentioned, it would be unlikely to reach him.

If proceedings are pending in the divorce registry which are treated as pending in a divorce county court, a document which is to be served by bailiff must be sent for service to the registrar of the county court within the district of which the document is to be served (r 120).

2 Petitions

Every matrimonial cause is begun by petition (r 8(1)), and the service of petitions is governed by r 14.

There are two exceptions to r 14, namely service on a person under disability (see below) and service out of England and Wales (see Chapter 16, head 5). Otherwise, the general rule is that 'a copy of every petition shall be served personally or by post on every respondent or co-respondent' (r 14(1)).

Except where the person to be served is under a disability, service may be effected either through the court or, where the petitioner requests, through the petitioner (r 14(2)(b)). However, the petitioner himself may not serve the petition personally (r 14(3)).

A copy of a petition to be served through the court must be served by post by an officer of the court, or if on a request by the petitioner the registrar so directs, by a bailiff delivering a copy to the party personally. A written request for bailiff service should be in Form D379 (see Form 22 in Appendix 2).

By r 13(1), a named adulterer with the respondent is made a co-respondent (and must be served) unless the court otherwise directs, or unless the respondent raped the named woman. In the latter case she will not be joined unless the court directs otherwise (r 13(2)). By r 13(3), where a petition alleges that the respondent has been guilty of an improper association, other than adultery, with a named person, the court may direct that that person be made a co-respondent. Notice of the hearing for directions is given to the petitioner and any person who has given notice of intention to defend. For a girl under sixteen years, see Persons under disability below.

A copy of the petition is deemed to be duly served if an acknowledgement of service in Form 6 (MCR Appendix 1) is signed by the party to be served or by a solicitor on his behalf, and is returned to the court office; and, where the form purports to be signed by the respondent, his signature is proved at the hearing (r 14(5)).

When an acknowledgement of service has been returned, the registrar sends a photocopy of it to the petitioner (r 14(8)).

If no acknowledgement of service has been returned, the registrar may nevertheless direct that the petition shall be deemed to have been served if he is satisfied by affidavit or otherwise that the respondent has in fact received the document (r 14(6)).

In the case of personal service (where no acknowledgement of service has been returned), service is proved by filing an affidavit of service, *or*, in the case of bailiff service, by an indorsement of service under CCR Ord 7, r 6(1)(*a*) (see Appendix 2, Form 17); *and* showing, in the case of a respondent, the server's means of knowledge of the identity of the party served (r 14(7)). Identification may be made by using a photograph of the respondent, by someone who knows him pointing him out to the process server or by the respondent admitting his identity.

By r 121(1), where a petition is sent to any person by an officer of the court he must record the date of posting and the address written on the letter or as the case may be, the number of the box at the document exchange and must sign a record and add the name of the court or registry to which he is attached. That record is evidence of the facts stated in the petition (r 121(2)).

Rule 14(9) provides that an application for leave to substitute some other mode of service for the mode of service prescribed by r 14(1), or to substitute notice of the proceedings by advertisement or otherwise, must be made ex parte by lodging an affidavit setting out the grounds on which the application is made. The form of advertisement is settled by the registrar. However, no order giving leave to substitute notice of the proceedings by advertisement may be made unless it appears to the registrar that there is a reasonable probability that the advertisement will come to the knowledge of the person concerned (ibid).

Further, where the court has authorised notice by advertisement to be substituted for service and the advertisement has been inserted by some person other than the registrar, that person must file copies of the newspapers containing the advertisements (r 121(3)).

CCR Ord 7, r 8(2) (see Chapter 9, head 4) applies in relation to bailiff service of a petition as it does to a county court summons (r 14(10)).

By r 14(11), where in the opinion of the registrar it is impracticable to serve a party in accordance with r 14(1)–(10), or it is otherwise necessary or expedient to dispense with service of a copy of a petition on the respondent or on any other person, the registrar may make an order dispensing with such service. An application for such an order must, if no notice of intention to defend has been given, be made in the first instance ex parte by lodging an affidavit setting out the grounds of the application, but the registrar may, if he thinks fit, require the attendance of the petitioner on the application (ibid). For form of affidavit, see Appendix 2, Form 23.

The affidavit must state all the enquiries which have been made concerning the respondent's whereabouts, and strenuous efforts will have to have been made before service will be dispensed with. Government departments may sometimes be used to trace the respondent (*Practice Direction* [1973] 1 WLR 60).

Where a petition or answer contains a charge of adultery by a husband with a minor girl under sixteen years of age, an application should be made to a registrar for directions as to whether she should be made a co-respondent and served (*Practice Direction* [1961] 1 All ER 129).

Persons under disability

Where a document to which r 14 applies is required to be served on a minor, r 113(1) provides that it is to be served on his father or guardian or, if he has no father or guardian, on the person with whom he resides or in whose care he is. Where such a document is required to be served on a patient (including a patient who is a minor) the document must be served:

(a) on the person (if any) who is authorised under the Mental Health Act 1983, Pt VII, to conduct in the name of the patient or on his behalf the proceedings in connection with which the document is to be served; or

(b) if there is no person so authorised, on the Official Solicitor if he has consented under r 112(5) to be the guardian ad litem of the patient, or

(c) in any other case, on the person with whom he resides or in whose care he is (usually the physician superintendent at the patient's hospital).

However, the court may order that a document which has been, or is to be, served on the person under disability or on a person other than one mentioned above be deemed to be duly served on the person under disability (ibid).

Where a document is served in accordance with r 113(1), it must be indorsed with a notice in Form 24 (MCR Appendix 1); and after service has been effected the person at whose instance the document was served must, unless the Official Solicitor is the guardian ad litem of the person under disability or the court otherwise directs, file an affidavit by the person on whom the document was served stating whether the contents of the document were, or its purport was, communicated to the person under disability and, if not, the reasons for not doing so (r 113(2)).

See r 112 for persons under disability suing through a next friend, and for notes on service in High Court proceedings, see Chapter 5, head 8.

3 Other proceedings

In the following proceedings, the foregoing rules as to the service of petitions apply mutatis mutandis:

- (*a*) originating applications under MCA, s 27 (wilful neglect to maintain) (r 98);
- (*b*) originating applications under MCA, ss 35 or 36 (alteration of maintenance agreement) (r 103(2));
- (*c*) originating summonses (High Court) under the Married Women's Property Act 1882, s 17 (r 104(12));
- (*d*) originating summonses (High Court) under the Matrimonial Homes Act 1983, ss 1 and 9 (r 107(1)).

Service of originating applications in the county court under the Married Women's Property Act 1882, s 17, the Matrimonial Homes Act 1983, ss 1 and 9, and the Inheritance (Provision for Family and Dependents) Act 1975 are governed by the ordinary CCR for serving originating applications (for which see Chapter 11, head 1).

A High Court originating summons under the Inheritance etc Act 1975 is served in accordance with RSC Ord 10, r 1. Note that the 1975 Act applies only to deaths after 1 April 1976; for prior deaths, see *Rayden on Divorce* (15th ed).

4 Subsequent pleadings

A supplemental or amended petition, together with a copy of the order giving leave to file the same, must be served on every respondent and co-respondent in the same manner as a petition is served (r 17(8), (9)).

A party filing an answer, reply or subsequent pleading must at the same time file a copy for service on every opposite party by the registrar (r 23).

Where any pleading subsequent to a petition makes allegations of adultery or improper association with a person, it is served, as is a petition, subject to r 13 (see head 2 above).

5 Orders

By r 59(1) where an order made in matrimonial proceedings has been drawn up, the registrar must, unless otherwise directed, send a copy of the order to every party affected by it.

Where a party against whom the order is made is acting by a solicitor, a copy may, if the registrar thinks fit, be sent to that party as if he were acting in person, as well as to his solicitor (r 59(2)).

It is not necessary for the person in whose favour the order was made to prove that a copy of the order has reached any other party to whom it is required to be sent (r 59(3)).

Rule 59 is without prejudice to RSC Ord 45, r 7 (which deals with the service of an order to do or abstain from doing an act: see Chapter 3, head 3. CCR Ord 29, r 1, as amended, which deals with orders enforceable by committal: see Chapter 12, head 10, and any other rule or enactment for the purposes of which an order is required to be served in a particular way (r 59(4)).

6 Summonses and notices

In matrimonial proceedings, those applications which are made by summons in the High Court, or on notice in a divorce county court, are served as follows.

In the High Court, the summons is served in accordance with RSC Ord 32, r 3 (see Chapter 3, head 9) and the mode of service, generally, is as in rr 118 and 119 (see head 1 above).

Where a summons is taken out by a spouse to apply for a decree nisi which has been made against him to be made absolute, four clear days' notice of the hearing must be given (r 66(2)). Fourteen days' notice of the return date must be given on a summons for an attachment of earnings order (RSC Ord 105, r 13(3)).

Where the proceedings are pending in a divorce county court, an application on notice is served in accordance with CCR Ord 13, r 1, giving two clear days' notice of the hearing (r 122). As in the

High Court (above) an application for a decree absolute under r 66 requires four days' notice. For the mode of service generally, see rr 118 and 119 (head 1 above).

Where an order under r 30 for the medical inspection of the parties to a nullity suit has been made, notice of the time and place of the appointment for the respondent's examination must be served on him (r 30(10)) according to rr 118 and 119 (see head 1 above).

7 Motions

Certain applications are by motion: eg for leave to issue a writ of sequestration, an appeal to the Divisional Court, or an appeal or application to the Court of Appeal. For service of those motions, see Chapter 2.

A motion by the Queen's Proctor to rescind a decree nisi where no answer has been filed to his plea, or where an answer has been filed and struck out or is not proceeded with, is served by him on every party affected by the proposed rescission and dismissal (r 61(5)).

8 Judgment summonses

A matrimonial judgment summons in Form 17 (MCR Appendix 1) must be served personally on the debtor not less than ten clear days before the hearing; at the time of service there must be paid or tendered to the debtor a sum reasonably sufficient to cover his expenses in travelling to and from the court at which he is summoned to appear (r 87(5)). See also CCR Ord 28, rr 2, 3 (Chapter 12, head 13).

CCR Ord 28, r 3(3) (successive judgment summonses) applies to a matrimonial judgment summons issued in either the High Court or a divorce county court, with the substitution of the words 'at the address stated in Form 16' (MCR Appendix 1) for the words 'within the district' (r 87(6)).

9 Applications for ancillary relief

Within four days after filing a notice of application for ancillary relief in Form 11, or under r 57 in Form 12 (MCR Appendix 1) the applicant must serve a copy on the respondent to the application.

A copy of the application in Form 11 or 13 together with a copy of the supporting affidavit must be served on the following persons in addition to the respondent to the application:

(a) in the case of an application for an order for a variation of settlement order, the trustees of the settlement and the settlor if living;

(b) in the case of an application for an order for an avoidance of disposition order, the person in whose favour the disposition is alleged to have been made;

(c) in the case of an application for a property adjustment order or an avoidance of disposition order relating to land, any mortgagee of whom particulars are given under r 74(3);

and such other persons, if any, as the registrar may direct (r 74(4)).

Any person so served may file an affidavit in answer within 14 days after service (r 74(6)).

Part II

Service out of the Jurisdiction

Chapter 14

Service out of the Jurisdiction without Leave

On 1 January 1987, the Civil Jurisdiction and Judgments Act 1982 came into force. In consequence, the provisions of RSC, Ord 11 and CCR, Ord 8 were substantially amended with effect from that date. Major changes in the law as to service out of the jurisdiction have been brought about—in summary, in very many cases originating process may now be served outside the jurisdiction without obtaining the leave of the court.

The 1982 Act incorporates into the law of the United Kingdom the amended 1968 Convention on Jurisdiction and the Enforcement of Judgments in Civil and Commercial Matters; the Convention is set out in the Schedules to the Act. The legislation, on its passage through Parliament, was rightly described as extremely complex. This book cannot set out the whole text of all the relevant provisions, and reference should be made to the Act where necessary.

The Act applies to the following countries: Belgium, Denmark, France, Federal Republic of Germany, Italy, Luxembourg, Netherlands, Republic of Ireland, United Kingdom.

High Court

The rules as to service of a writ out of the jurisdiction without leave are contained in Ord 11, r 1(2). There are a number of situations covered:

(*a*) Each claim made by the writ is a claim which by virtue of the 1982 Act the court has power to hear and determine, made in proceedings to which the following conditions apply:

(i) no proceedings between the parties concerning the same cause of action are pending in the courts of any other part of the United Kingdom or of any other Convention territory, and

109

    (ii) either the defendant is domiciled in any part of the United Kingdom or in any other Convention territory, *or* the proceedings begun by the writ are proceedings to which art 16 of Sched 1 or of Sched 4 refers, or the defendant is a party to an agreement conferring jurisdiction to which art 17 of Sched 1 or of Sched 4 to the 1982 Act applies; or

(*b*) Each claim made by the writ is a claim which by virtue of any other enactment the High Court has power to hear and determine notwithstanding that the person against whom the claim is made is not within the jurisdiction of the court or that the wrongful act, neglect or default giving rise to the claim did not take place within its jurisdiction.

It is necessary to consider the requirements of paragraph (*a*).

1 Jurisdiction

The court must have jurisdiction under the Act to deal with the claim.

The Convention as amended, set out in the Schedules to the Act, applies, subject to exceptions, to all civil and commercial matters, whatever the nature of the court or tribunal. The exceptions are revenue, customs and administrative matters, cases involving status or legal capacity, matrimonial property, wills and succession, all insolvency matters, social security and arbitration (Sched 1, art 1).

Jurisdiction is dealt with in arts 2–24 of Sched 1. By art 2, unless one of the alternative provisions as to jurisdiction applies, *persons must, whatever their nationality, be sued in the courts of the state in which they are domiciled.* Persons who are not nationals of the state in which they are domiciled are governed by the rules of jurisdiction applicable to nationals of that state. Domicile will be considered in the next section.

By art 3, persons domiciled in one state may be sued in the courts of another state only by virtue of the rules set out in arts 5–18. Jurisdiction may no longer be founded on:

(*a*) the document instituting the proceedings having been served on the defendant during his temporary presence in the UK;

(*b*) the presence in the UK of property belonging to the defendant; or

(*c*) the seizure by the plaintiff of property situated in the UK.

Articles 5–18 are too lengthy to be set out in full, and reference should be made to the Act if necessary. Article 5 provides that a person domiciled in a contracting state may, in another contracting state, be sued:

(a) in contract, in the court of the place of performance of the obligation in question;

(b) in maintenance, in the court for the place where the maintenance creditor is domiciled or habitually resident;

(c) in tort, in the court for the place where the harmful event occurred;

(d) where a civil claim arises from a criminal act, in the court dealing with the criminal proceedings where that court has civil jurisdiction;

(e) where a dispute arises out of the operation of a branch or agency, in the court where the branch is established;

(f) in trust matters, in the court where the trust is domiciled (see 1982 Act, s 45);

(g) in salvage matters, in the court which authorised the arrest.

Article 6 provides that a person domiciled in a contracting state may also be sued:

(a) where he is one of a number of defendants, in the courts for the place where any one of them is domiciled;

(b) as a third party, in the court seised of the original proceedings, unless these were instituted solely with the object of removing him from the jurisdiction of the court which would be competent in his case;

(c) on a counterclaim arising from the same contract or facts on which the original claim was based, in the court in which the original claim is pending.

Articles 7–12A deal with jurisdiction in insurance cases, and should be referred to in full. In summary, a policy-holder plaintiff has a wide choice of courts, but an insurer plaintiff may only sue in the court of policy-holder's domicile. The parties may only agree to depart from the rules if strict rules are complied with (arts 12 and 12A).

Articles 13–15 deal with jurisdiction over consumer contracts, and are similar in effect to the rules relating to insurance claims. Essentially, a consumer plaintiff may sue the supplier etc in the courts of his or the supplier's domicile (which includes a contracting state where the supplier has a branch). However, the consumer may only be sued in the place where he is domiciled. Article 15 provides for an agreement to depart from the general rule only where certain conditions are complied with.

2 Domicile

By virtue of Arts 52 and 53 in Sched 1 to the 1982 Act, each contracting state applies its own law to determine the domicile of a person within that state. For the UK, domicile is defined in ss 41–46 of the Act.

(a) Individuals

An individual is domiciled in the UK if and only if:
- (a) he is resident in the UK; and
- (b) the nature and circumstances of his residence indicate that he has a substantial connection with the UK (s 41(2)).

It is, of course, necessary to know whether the defendant is domiciled in England and Wales on the one hand, or in Scotland or Northern Ireland on the other hand.

Section 41(3) provides that, subject to subs (5), an individual is domiciled in a particular part of the UK if and only if:
- (a) he is resident in that part; and
- (b) the nature and circumstances of his residence indicate that he has a substantial connection with that part.

Subsection (5) provides that an individual who is domiciled in the UK but does not have a substantial connection with any particular part of the UK shall be treated as domiciled in the part in which he is resident.

The concept of 'place' of domicile is relevant to some of the provisions as to jurisdiction referred to above. By s 41(4), an individual is domiciled in a particular place in the UK if and only if he:
- (a) is domiciled in the part of the UK in which that place is situated; and
- (b) is resident in that place.

So far as 'substantial connection' is concerned in relation to domicile in the UK or part thereof, s 41(6) provides for a rebuttable presumption that the test is satisfied if the individual has been resident in the UK or a particular part for at least three months.

In relation to domicile in a state other than a contracting state, s 41(7) states that an individual is domiciled if and only if:
- (a) he is resident in that state; and
- (b) the nature and circumstances of his residence indicate that

he has a substantial connection with the state. The three months presumption in s 41(6) does not apply in this case.

(b) Corporations and associations

This is dealt with in ss 42 and 43. The seat of a corporation or association is treated as its domicile (s 42(1)). Section 42 defines the seat for almost all purposes (s 42(2)). A corporation means a body corporate and includes a Scottish partnership, and an association means an unincorporated body of persons (s 50).

A corporation or association has its seat in the UK if and only if:

(a) it was incorporated or formed under the law of a part of the UK and has its registered office or some other official address in the UK; or

(b) its central management and control is exercised in the UK (s 42(3)).

'Official address' is defined by s 42(8) as meaning an address which it is required by law to register, notify or maintain for the purpose of receiving notices or other communications.

A corporation has its seat in a particular *part* of the UK [ie in England and Wales, or Scotland or Northern Ireland] if and only if it has its seat in the UK and:

(a) it has its registered office or some other official address in that part; or

(b) its central management and control is exercised in that part; or

(c) it has a place of business in that part (s 42(4)).

'Business' includes any activity carried on by a corporation or association, and 'place of business' shall be construed accordingly (s 42(8)).

A corporation or association has its seat in a particular *place* in the UK if and only if it has its seat in the part of the UK in which that place is situated and:

(a) it has its registered office or some other official address in that place; or

(b) it has a place of business in that place.

By s 42(6), a corporation or association has its seat in a state other than the UK if and only if:

(a) it was incorporated or formed under the law of that state and has its registered office or some other official address there; or

(b) its central management and control is exercised in that state.

However, in relation to another *contracting* state, the courts of that state must regard the corporation or association as having its seat there (s 42(7)).

Section 43 of the Act defines 'seat' in respect of those articles which deal with the jurisdiction of cases concerning the formation, dissolution, constitution etc. of corporations etc. Reference should be made to s 43.

(c) Others

Section 44 of the Act deals with the deemed domicile of parties to insurance and insurance contracts under arts 8 and 13, mentioned above. The insurer or supplier of goods is treated as domiciled in the part of the UK where his branch, etc is situated.

By s 45, a trust is domiciled in the UK if and only if it is domiciled in a part of the UK (s 45(2)). It is domiciled in a part of the UK if and only if the system of law of that part is the system of law with which the trust has its closest and most real connection.

Section 46 deals with the domicile and seat of the Crown. Reference should be made to the Act.

3 Article 16 etc

Referring back to Ord 11, r 1(2)(a), the alternative to the requirement of domicile in any part of the UK or in any other Convention territory is that the proceedings are those to which certain provisions in the Convention apply.

Article 16 of Sched 1 provides that the following courts shall have *exclusive jurisdiction, regardless of domicile*:

(1) in proceedings which have as their object rights in rem in, or tenancies of, immovable property, the courts of the contracting state in which the property is situated;

(2) in proceedings which have as their object the validity of the constitution, the nullity or the dissolution of companies or other legal persons or associations of natural or legal persons, or the decisions of their organs, the courts of the Contracting State in which the register is kept;

(3) in proceedings which have as their object the validity of entries in public registers, the courts of the Contracting State in which the register is kept;

(4) in proceedings concerned with the registraton or validity of patents, trade marks, designs, or other similar rights required to be deposited or registered, the courts of the Contracting State in which the deposit or registration has been applied for, has taken place or

is under the terms of an international convention deemed to have taken place;

(5) in proceedings concerned with the enforcement of judgments, the courts of the Contracting State in which the judgment has been or is to be enforced.

It should be noted that the parties cannot contract out of art 16 and, by art 19, if a case falling within art 16 comes before the wrong court, that court must decline jurisdiction of its own motion.

Schedule 4 deals with claims against persons domiciled in one part of the UK being sued in another part of the UK. The Convention was modified for the allocation of jurisdiction within the UK. Though the framework is similar to Sched 1, there are certain differences, and Sched 4 should be referred to, where necessary.

Agreement to confer jurisdiction By art 17 of Sched 1, if the parties, one or more of whom is domicilied in a contracting state, have agreed that a court or the courts of a contracting state are to have jurisdiction to settle any disputes which have arisen or which may arise in connection with a particular legal relationship, that court or those courts shall have exclusive jurisdiction.

The agreement must be:

(*a*) in writing; or

(*b*) evidenced in writing; or

(*c*) in international trade or commerce, in a form which accords with practices in that trade or commerce of which the parties are or ought to have been aware.

Where such agreement is concluded by parties, none of whom is domiciled in a contracting state, the courts of other contracting states have no jurisdiction over their disputes unless the court(s) chosen have declined jurisdiction.

If an agreement conferring jurisdiction was concluded for the benefit of only one of the parties, that party retains the right to bring proceedings in any other court which has jurisdiction by virtue of the Convention.

The court(s) of a contracting state on which a trust instrument has conferred jurisdiction have exclusive jurisdiction in any proceedings brought against a settlor, trustee or beneficiary, if relations between these persons or their rights or obligations under the trust are involved. However, the terms of a trust instrument cannot confer jurisdiction in insurance or consumer contracts to which arts 12 and 15 apply, nor can they override art 16.

Schedule 4, art 17 provides, in respect of jurisdiction between different parts of the UK, a modified and less stringent version of the requirements for an agreement from that set out in art 17 of Sched 1.

Entering an appearance By Art 18, apart from jurisdiction derived from any other provision, a court of a contracting state has jurisdiction by virtue of the defendant entering an appearance (ie by acknowledging service and giving notice of intention to defend), unless the appearance was entered solely to contest the jurisdiction, or where another court has exclusive jurisdiction by virtue of art 16.

Procedure

By virtue of Practice Direction [1987] 1 WLR 86, and RSC Ord 6, r 7, the writ to be served out of the jurisdiction without leave must be indorsed, before issue, with a statement that the High Court of England and Wales has the power under the Civil Jurisdiction and Judgments Act 1982 to hear and determine the claim and that no proceedings are pending between the parties in Scotland, Northern Ireland or another convention territory of any contracting state.

Where the writ is to be served abroad, the number of days for acknowledging service under the extra-jurisdiction table (see Appendix 1) must be stated on the writ (Practice Direction, para 6). For service in Scotland, Northern Ireland or in the European territory of another contracting state, the time is 21 days; for service under r 1(2)(a) in any other territory of a contracting state, the time is 31 days; otherwise in accordance with the extra-jurisdiction table (r 1(3)).

By Ord 11, r 9, the same rules as to service without leave apply to an originating summons, notice of motion and petition.

For the rules as to effecting service, see Chapter 15.

County court

CCR Ord 8, r 2(2) is in the same terms as RSC Ord 11, r 1(2) save that the words 'an originating process' replace the words 'a writ'. Where the originating process is in a default action, the time fixed for delivering an admission or defence or paying the total amount of the claim and costs into court, is the same as the time for acknowledgement of service in Ord 11, r 1(3)(CCR Ord 8, r 2(3)). In a fixed date action, the court fixes the return date having regard to the distance of the country of service.

By Ord 8, r 4, service of an interlocutory process out of England and Wales is permissible with leave of the court on a person who is already a party to the proceedings and, in the case of a defendant, respondent or third party, has been served with the originating process but leave shall not be required for such service in any proceedings in which the originating process may be these rules or under any Act to be served out of England and Wales without leave.

Examples

(1) A motor accident takes place in England between a French national (on holiday in England), who is domiciled in Italy and a Scot, also a tourist. The Scot wishes to bring proceedings for damages in the English High Court.

The Scot may issue proceedings in England and serve them, without leave, on the Frenchman in Italy, provided no other proceedings have been started arising out of the same incident. By art 5(3) of Sched 1, the English court has jurisdiction because the harmful event occurred in England.

(2) A dispute arises as to the tenancy of a farm in Belgium, between the owner of the land, who is domiciled in England, and the tenant, who is domiciled in the Netherlands. The owner brings proceedings for possession of the land in the English High Court and wishes to serve the tenant in the Netherlands.

By art 16 of Sched 1, only the Belgian courts have jurisdiction to hear the dispute and the High Court must decline jurisdiction of its own motion.

Chapter 15

The Court's Discretion

In cases not covered by Ord 11, r 1(2), as dealt with in Chapter 14, it is necessary to obtain the leave of the court to serve the writ or other originating process out of the jurisdiction. Chapters 16 and 17 deal with the procedure.

This chapter details the cases where an application to serve process out of the jurisdiction may be made and concludes with a section on how the courts exercise their discretion in the matter. It must be remembered that this book can only give an outline of the authorities under each heading. For a more detailed analysis reference should be made to Dicey and Morris on *The Conflict of Laws* (11th ed, 1987).

1 Applications within RSC Ord 11, r 1(1), or CCR Ord 8, r 2

RSC Ord 11, r 1(1) provides that:

Provided that the writ does not contain any claim mentioned on Order 75, r 2(1) [*for which see head 2 below*] and is not a writ to which paragraph (2) of this rule applies [*see Chapter 14*], service of a writ out of the jurisdiction is permissible with the leave of the Court if in the action begun by the writ . . .

CCR Ord 8, r 2(1) provides that:

Except in an action to which paragraph (2) [*for which see Chapter 14*] or rule 3 [*see head 2 below*] applies, service of an originating process out of England and Wales is permissible with the leave of the court where . . .

Each of the 19 sub-paragraphs ((a)–(s)) in Ord 11, r 1(1) is set out below in sequence followed by an explanatory passage where this is necessary. In CCR Ord 8, r 2(1), there are 15 cases in the list of county court actions where leave may be sought (paras (a)–(o)).

The categories in both High Court and county court were substantially redrafted at the same time as the rules were altered in respect of the 1982 Act. The wording of the equivalent rules in the county court follows the High Court rules much more closely than before. Any differences in the County Court Rules are noted in each case. The principles in deciding whether to grant leave are the same for both jurisdictions.

> (*a*) relief is sought against a person domiciled within the jurisdiction [*wording in CCR is the same, save that the last three words are replaced by 'in England and Wales'*].

By RSC Ord 11, r 1(4) and CCR Ord 8, r 2(5), domicile is to be determined in accordance with the provisions of ss 41–46 of the Civil Jurisdiction and Judgments Act 1982, as to which see the section on Domicile in Chapter 14.

> (*b*) an injunction is sought ordering the defendant to do or refrain from doing anything within the jurisdiction (whether or not damages are also claimed in respect of a failure to do or the doing of that thing) [*wording in CCR is the same, save that the words 'within the jurisdiction' are omitted*].

In exercising its discretion under this paragraph, the court will consider the following:

(1) An injunction must be the substantial (though not necessarily the sole) relief sought. If a claim for an injunction is merely tagged on in order to bring a cause of action within the paragraph, leave will be refused (*De Bernales* v *New York Herald* (1893) 62 LJQB 385).

(2) There must be some method of making the injunction effective within the jurisdiction (*Marshall* v *Marshall* (1888) 38 Ch D 330).

(3) There must be evidence of the likelihood of a repetition of the alleged wrong (*Watson & Sons* v *Daily Record (Glasgow) Ltd* [1907] 1 KB 853).

(4) The court will refuse leave if a foreign court is the more convenient forum to deal with the case (*Rosler* v *Hilbery* [1925] Ch 250 and see head 3 below).

In *The Siskina* [1979] AC 210, the House of Lords held that a claim for the interlocutory relief of a Mareva injunction did not fall within the paragraph where the substantive cause of action did not come within any of the categories of Ord 11, r 1. It should be noted that s 24 and 25 of the 1982 Act have modified this decision where proceedings are or have been commenced in another contracting state; see also *Republic of Haiti* v *Duvalier* [1989] 2 WLR 261.

(*c*) the claim is brought against a person duly served within or out of the jurisdiction and a person out of the jurisdiction is a necessary or proper party thereto [*CCR equivalent has 'the jurisdiction' replaced by 'England and Wales'*].

By Ord 11, r 4(1)(d) and CCR Ord 8, r 6(1)(b)(iv), the affidavit in support of an application for leave under this rule must contain, inter alia, the grounds for the deponent's belief that there is between the plaintiff and the person on whom the proceedings have been served a real issue which the plaintiff may reasonably ask the court to try. This is to prevent the plaintiff from not acting bona fide in joining the original defendant, simply in order to serve the other person out of the jurisdiction under para (*c*).

Under RSC Ord 16, r 3(4) leave may be granted under (*c*) to serve a third party notice outside the jurisdiction on any necessary or proper party to the proceedings brought against the defendant.

(*d*) the claim is brought to enforce, rescind, dissolve, annul or otherwise affect a contract, or to recover damages or obtain other relief in respect of the breach of a contract, being (in either case) a contract which—
  (i) was made within the jurisdiction, or
  (ii) was made by or through an agent trading or residing within the jurisdiction on behalf of a principal trading or residing out of the jurisdiction, or
  (iii) is by its terms, or by implication, governed by English law, or
  (iv) contains a term to the effect that the High Court shall have jurisdiction to hear and determine any action in respect of the contract.

The county court provision relating to contract is considered in connection with (e) below.

'Contract' includes an implied or quasi-contract (*Bowling* v *Cox* [1926] AC 751), and an alleged contract where the plaintiff has a good arguable case that one existed.

The words 'or otherwise affect a contract' include a claim for a declaration that a contract has become discharged as a result of frustration (*BP Exploration Co (Libya) Ltd* v *Hunt* [1976] 1 WLR 788).

Under (i), the contract must be made within the jurisdiction. Since 'contract' includes 'quasi-contract', the word 'made' should be read as 'arising' when describing a quasi-contract (*Ronson's Trustee* v *Ronson* [1955] 3 All ER 486).

Where a contract is negotiated by correspondence, it is 'made' in the country where the letter of acceptance is posted or from where a telegram of acceptance is sent. Where a telex, telephone or other immediate form of communication is employed, the contract is 'made' where the acceptance is received by the offeror (*Entores Ltd* v *Miles Far East Corporation* [1955] 2 QB 327, applied in *Brinkibon Ltd* v *Stahag Stahl GmbH* [1983] 2 AC 341, HL).

Where a contract made within the jurisdiction is amended by an agreement made outside the jurisdiction, the amended contract will be deemed to have been made within, unless it, in effect, substitutes a new agreement, and this will always be a question of degree in each case (*BP Exploration Co (Libya) Ltd* v *Hunt* (above)). On the other hand, a contract made within the jurisdiction, though preceded by an informal agreement made outside, is within the paragraph (*Gibbon* v *Commerz und Creditbank A/G* [1958] 2 Lloyd's Rep 113).

An action in England to enforce a foreign arbitration award under a contract made in England which provided that any dispute should be settled by arbitration in Hamburg was held to be within the paragraph (*Bremer Oeltransport GmbH* v *Drewry* [1933] 1 KB 753).

Under (ii), the contract was made 'through an agent' even though the agent had no authority to enter into contracts, but only to negotiate, and the contract was actually concluded by the principal abroad (*National Mortgage and Agency Company of New Zealand* v *Gosselin* (1922) 38 TLR 832). Compare RSC Ord 10, r 2 (Chapter 5, head 9).

Paragraph (iii) means that English law is the 'proper law' of the contract, and is discussed fully in Dicey and Morris. Essentially, the expression means the system of law by which the parties intended the contract to be governed, or, where their intention is neither expressed nor to be inferred from the circumstances, the system of law with which the transaction has its closest and most real connection (ibid, p 747).

In *Matthews* v *Kuwait Bechtel Corporation* [1959] 2 QB 57, it was held that where a plaintiff had an alternative remedy in contract or in tort, he could choose his remedy and obtain leave under this paragraph.

Paragraph (iv) contains the provision which was formerly dealt with in Ord 11, r 2.

    (*e*) the claim is brought in respect of a breach committed within the jurisdiction of a contract made within or out of the jurisdiction, and irrespective of the fact, if such be the case, that the breach was preceded or accompanied by a breach committed out of the jurisdiction that rendered impossible the performance of so much of the contract as ought to have been performed within the jurisdiction.

The county court equivalent is:

(d) the claim is founded on any breach or alleged breach of any contract wherever made, which—
 (i) according to its terms ought to be performed in England and Wales, or
 (ii) is by its terms, or by implication, governed by English law, or
 (iii) contains a term to the effect that a court in England or Wales shall have jurisdiction to hear and determine any action in respect of the contract.

Dicey and Morris deals with this provision in detail. No breach can be committed within the jurisdiction (so as to come within this paragraph) unless a contractual obligation has to be performed within the jurisdiction (*Cuban Atlantic Sugar Sales Corpn* v *Compania de Vapores San Elefterio Limitada* [1960] 1 QB 187). Where a letter of repudiation is the breach of contract, the breach occurs in the country where the letter was posted (*Holland* v *Bennett* [1902] 1 KB 867).

If the contract does not specify where payment must be made (either expressly or impliedly), the debtor has a duty to seek out the creditor, and if the latter is within the jurisdiction the breach falls within this paragraph.

(f) the claim is founded on a tort and the damage was sustained, or resulted from an act committed, within the jurisdiction [*the county court equivalent is in para (e) and the words 'the jurisdiction' are replaced by 'England and Wales'*].

The recent case of *Metall und Rohstoff AG* v *Donaldson Lufkin & Jenrette* [1989] 3 WLR 563 is the first decision of the Court of Appeal to consider the present form of this paragraph. It is an important decision, and leave to appeal to the House of Lords has been granted. The following principles are laid down:

(i) The court would only assume jurisdiction where the claim was founded on a tort and either the damage was sustained within the jurisdiction or the damage resulted from an act committed within the jurisdiction;
(ii) Where damage had occurred in more than one jurisdiction then the court would assume jurisdiction if significant

damage had occurred within the jurisdiction, or, where the tort consisted of acts done in more than one jurisdiction, where substantial acts had been committed within the court's jurisdiction;

(iii) Where a person by acts committed abroad had caused injury or damage to a person in England, the court had first to consider whether by reference exclusively to English law, it could properly be said that a tort had been committed in substance within the jurisdiction of the English courts;

(iv) If the tort had in substance been committed within the jurisdiction, the court would assume jurisdiction;

(v) If the tort was in substance committed abroad, the court's jurisdiction would be limited to a case where the relevant acts would give rise to a tort actionable both in the foreign jurisdiction and in English law;

(vi) A claim founded on a constructive trust or procuring a breach of trust was not a tort within (*f*).

(*g*) the whole subject-matter of the action is land situate within the jurisdiction (with or without rents or profits) or the perpetuation of testimony relating to land so situate [*the county court equivalent is (*f*), omitting the words 'within the jurisdiction'*].

This includes a claim for possession of land (*Agnew* v *Usher* (1884) 14 QBD 78, per Lord Coleridge CJ at p 79). In an Irish case, *Clare County Council* v *Wilson* [1913] 2 IR 89, it was held that an action to recover extraordinary expenses necessary for repairing roads damaged by excessive user, under the Public Roads (Ireland) Act 1911, did not come within any of the categories in RSC Ord 11, r 1.

(*h*) the claim is brought to construe, rectify, set aside or enforce an act, deed, will, contract, obligation or liability affecting land situate within the jurisdiction [*the county court equivalent is (*g*), omitting the words 'within the jurisdiction'*].

The courts have held that the following cases come within the paragraph:

(*a*) where the action was for breach of a covenant to repair by the assignee of a lease (*Tassell* v *Hallen* [1892] 1 QB 321);

(*b*) where an outgoing tenant claimed compensation for tenant right (improvement) according to the custom of the country (*Kaye* v *Sutherland* (1887) 20 QBD 147);

(*c*) where the claim was for a declaration that the defendants were trustees of certain lands and damages for breach of trust (*Attorney-General* v *Drapers Company* [1894] 1 IR 185); and

(*d*) where the claim was for the proceeds of the sale of land held under a trust, even though the land had been sold and the proceeds were no longer within the jurisdiction (*Official Solicitor* v *Stype Investments (Jersey) Ltd* [1983] 1 WLR 214,

and that the following fall outside it:

(i) a claim for rent againt an alleged assignee of premises (*Agnew* v *Usher* (1884) 14 QBD 78, though this has been interpreted narrowly in *Kaye* v *Sutherland* (above)); and

(ii) an action in the nature of slander of title (*Casey* v *Arnot* (1876) 2 CPD 24).

Cheshire and North's *Private International Law* concludes that the best general guide, derived from *Casey* v *Arnot* is that 'what is complained of must be something that directly affects the land itself, not something that merely affects its value'.

(*i*) the claim is made for a debt secured on immovable property or is made to assert, declare or determine proprietary or possessory rights, or rights of security, in or over movable property, or to obtain authority to dispose of movable property, situate within the jurisdiction [*the county court equivalent is para* (h) *omitting the words 'within the jurisdiction'*].

(*j*) the claim is brought to execute the trusts of a written instrument being trusts that ought to be executed according to English law and of which the person to be served with the writ is a trustee, or for any relief or remedy which might be obtained in any such action [*the county court equivalent is para* (i) *with the replacement of the word 'writ' by 'originating process'*].

Unlike the previous rule, it is now unnecessary for any trust property to be within the jurisdiction.

(*k*) the claim is made for the administration of the estate of a person who died domiciled within the jurisdiction or for any relief or remedy which might be obtained in any such action [*the county court equivalent is para* (j) *with the replacement of the words 'within the jurisdiction' by 'in England and Wales', and the words 'in any such action' by 'when such a claim is made'*].

As to the definition of domicile, see Chapter 14.

(*l*) the claim is brought in a probate action within the meaning of Order 76 [*the county court equivalent is para* (k) *referring to Ord 41*].

(*m*) the claim is brought to enforce any judgment or arbitral award [*the county court equivalent is para (l)*].

This paragraph fills a lacuna—see Supreme Court Practice, para 11/1/25.

(*n*) the claim is brought against a defendant not domiciled in Scotland or Northern Ireland in respect of a claim by the Commissioners of Inland Revenue for or in relation to any of the duties or taxes which have been, or are for the time being, placed under their care and management [*the county court equivalent is para (m)*]

(*o*) the claim is brought under the Nuclear Installations Act 1965 or in respect of contributions under the Social Security Act 1975 [*the county court equivalent in para (n) only covers the Social Security Act*].

(*p*) the claim is made for a sum to which the Directive of the Council of the European Communities dated 15th March 1976 No. 76/308/ EEC applies, and service is to be effected in a country which is a member State of the European Economic Community [*the county court equivalent is para (o)*].

This refers to claims by HM Customs and Excise for sums due under the European Agricultural Guidance and Guarantee Fund and for agricultural levies, customs duties and (through an amendment to the Directive dated 6 December 1979) value added tax.

(*q*) the claim is made under the Drug Trafficking Offences Act 1986 [*there is no county court equivalent*].

(*r*) the claim is made under the Banking Act 1987 [*there is no county court equivalent*].

(*s*) the claim is made under Part VI of the Criminal Justice Act 1988 [*there is no county court equivalent*].

This relates to the confiscation of the proceeds of a criminal offence.

2 Admiralty

In relation to admiralty actions as can be seen from the opening words of RSC Ord 11, r 1(1) service out of the jurisdiction under Ord 11 does *not* apply to claims mentioned in RSC Ord 75, r 2(1), ie actions to enforce a claim for damage, loss of life or personal injury arising out of:

(*a*) a collision between ships;

(*b*) the carrying out of or omission to carry out a manoeuvre in the case of one or more of two or more ships; or

(c) non-compliance, on the part of one or more of two or more ships, with the collision regulations;

(d) every limitation action; and

(e) every action to enforce a claim under s 1 of the Merchant Shipping (Oil Pollution) Act 1971 on s 4 of the Merchant Shipping Act 1974.

The procedure for service out of the jurisdiction in an admiralty action is governed by RSC Ord 75, r 4. It should be noted that, by virtue of RSC Ord 75, r 4(3), there is no provision for service out of the jurisdiction of an admiralty action in *rem*. The effect of r 4 is to permit service out of the jurisdiction in certain actions in *personam*, provided they are not contrary to the Supreme Court Act 1981, s 22.

Rule 4(1) provides that, subject to r 4(1A)–(4), service out of the jurisdiction of a writ containing any of the claims mentioned in Ord 75, r 2(1) ((a)–(d) above), is permissible with the leave of the court if, but only if:

(a) the defendant has his habitual residence or a place of business within England and Wales;

(b) the cause of action arose within inland waters of England and Wales or within the limits of a port of England and Wales;

(c) an action arising out of the same incident or incidents is proceeding in the High Court or has been heard and determined in the High Court; or

(d) the defendant has submitted or agreed to submit to the jurisdiction of the High Court.

In this paragraph 'inland waters' and 'port' have the same meanings as in the Supreme Court Act 1981, s 22. In every action to enforce a claim under the Merchant Shipping (Oil Pollution) Act 1971, s 1, or the Merchant Shipping Act 1974, s 4 (r 2(1)(c)), leave may be obtained to serve writ out of the jurisdiction: r 4 (1A).

An application for leave is made in the same way as an application under RSC Ord 11, r 4 (Ord 75, r 4(2)).

In the county court, equivalent provisions to the above are contained in the County Courts Act 1984, s 30, and CCR Ord 8, r 3, which are set out in the *County Court Practice*.

3 Exercise of the court's discretion

The wording of RSC Ord 11, r 1(1) is not mandatory, so that a plaintiff will not necessarily be granted leave to serve his writ out of the jurisdiction merely by coming within one of the specified categories. There have been numerous cases on how the court will exercise its discretion, many of them on a defendant's application to stay the proceedings once the process has been served. In such a case the same principles apply, though it must always be remembered that the onus of proof is reserved, ie, is on the defendant to show that the plaintiff should be deprived of the right to bring an action in England and Wales (*Spiliada Maritime Corpn v Cansulex Ltd* [1987] AC 460).

The following is a list of many of the factors which the court may take into account:

(1) The plaintiff must show that he has a 'good arguable case' on the merits (*Diamond v Bank of London and Montreal Ltd* [1979] QB 333). Both RSC Ord 11, r 4(2), and CCR Ord 8, r 6(2), require that the plaintiff must show that 'the case is a proper one' for service out of the jurisdiction. Two House of Lords decisions, *The Brabo* [1949] AC 326 and *Vitkovice Horni v Korner* [1951] AC 869, establish that the standard falls between showing a prima facie case and proof beyond reasonable doubt, and the expression 'good arguable case' is probably the most helpful.

(2) The case must 'fall within the spirit as well as the letter of the various classes of cases provided for [in RSC Ord 11]' (per Viscount Haldane in *Johnson v Taylor Bros & Co Ltd* [1920] AC 144, 153).

(3) If there is any doubt in construing RSC Ord 11, 'it ought to be resolved in favour of the foreigner,' (per Farwell LJ in *The Hagen* [1908] P 189, 201).

(4) 'It becomes a very serious question. . . whether this court ought to put a foreigner, who owes no allegiance here, to the inconvenience and annoyance of being brought to contest his rights in this country, and. . . this court ought to be exceedingly careful before it allows a writ to be served out of the jurisdiction' (per Pearson J in *Société Générale de Paris v Dreyfus Bros* (1885) 29 ChD 239, at pp 242–3). Quaere whether such extreme caution is appropriate in the days of relatively cheap air travel.

(5) Since the application is made by the plaintiff ex parte, 'full and fair disclosure is necessary' of all the relevant facts (per Farwell LJ in *The Hagen* (above) at p 201).

(6) '[A] plaintiff wishing to proceed under [RSC Ord 11] to

serve a defendant out of the jurisdiction should act with reasonable speed. Inordinate delay for no good reason is a strong factor to be taken into consideration in exercising the court's discretion' (per Kerr J in *The Nimrod* [1973] 2 Lloyd's Rep 91,96). In that case the writ was issued in December 1968; application for leave was made in May 1971; leave was refused.

(7) The court will consider which is the appropriate court to try the action (known as the 'forum conveniens') and will take into account, inter alia,

(a) which country's law governs the cause of action and where the most effective relief will be given. In particular, if the parties have agreed that a particular country's courts should have jurisdiction over a dispute, the court will not generally go behind that agreement (*Mackender* v *Feldia AG* [1967] 2 QB 590);

(b) whether a foreign court has jurisdiction and whether both parties would have a fair trial at that foreign court;

(c) where the witnesses reside and the places where the parties render or carry on business (*Spiliada Maritime Corpn* (above)).

(8) As a general consideration of the forum conveniens the court will compare the cost and convenience of the alternative jurisdictions. In applications for leave to serve process in Scotland and Northern Ireland, both the High Court (RSC Ord 11, r 4(3)) and county court (CCR Ord 8, r 5) are specifically directed to have regard to this comparison. They are further required to consider the powers and jurisdiction of the sheriff's or small debts courts in Scotland or the county courts or courts of summary jurisdiction in Northern Ireland.

(9) As has been mentioned, many disputes over jurisdiction arise when the defendant applies to set aside service when the onus is on him to show either that the court chosen was not the appropriate one (forum non conveniens) or that the issue in dispute is already being tried abroad (lis alibi pendens). The principles to be applied were fully canvassed in two recent House of Lords cases, *The Atlantic Star* [1974] AC 436 and *MacShannon* v *Rockware Glass Ltd* [1978] AC 795, and are fully discussed in detail in Chapter 12 of Dicey and Morris. The test is now as follows:

(i) 'A mere balance of convenience is not a sufficient

ground for depriving a plaintiff of the advantages of prosecuting his action in an English Court if it is otherwise properly brought. The right of access to the King's Court must not be lightly refused' (per Scott LJ in *St Pierre* v *South American Stores)Gath and Chaves) Ltd* [1936] 1 KB 382, 398 as applied in *MacShannon*).

(ii) 'In order to justify a stay two conditions must be satisfied, one positive and the other negative: (*a*) the defendant must satisfy the court that there is another forum to whose jurisdiction he is amenable in which justice can be done between the parties at substantially less inconvenience or expense, and (*b*) the stay must not deprive the plaintiff of a legitimate personal or judicial advantage which would be available to him if he invoked the jurisdiction of the English court' (per Lord Diplock in *MacShannon* at p 812, modifying the second part of Scott LJ's test in *St Pierre*).

The most recent decision of the House of Lords, *Spiliada Maritime Corp* v *Cansulex Ltd* [1987] AC 460 restates the principles, and the speech of Lord Goff is a clear statement of the law, to which reference should be made in *every* difficult case.

Chapter 16

High Court Process

This chapter deals with the procedure in the High Court for obtaining leave, in a case not falling within Chapter 14. The procedural rules are largely contained in RSC Ord 11. This chapter also deals with service of other originating process, service of amended writs and service on foreign states.

1 Application for leave to issue writ

An application for leave to issue a writ, as well as to serve it, out of the jurisdiction must be made where the defendant (or all of them, if there is more than one) is out of the jurisdiction, since RSC Ord 6, r 7(1), provides that no such writ may be issued without leave of the court. Where at least one defendant is within the jurisdiction an ordinary writ should be issued with the names and addresses of all the defendants and specially sealed with a notification that it is 'not for service out of the jurisdiction'. Thereafter a subsequent application should be made to issue a concurrent writ for service out of the jurisdiction, under RSC Ord 6, r 6. In the Queen's Bench Division the application is made ex parte to a master or district registrar under RSC Ord 32, r 11, or Ord 32, r 23, respectively.

The application for leave is made by affidavit, sworn by the plaintiff, his solicitor, or anyone who can swear to the facts. It must state the following:

    (*a*) the grounds on which the application is made; ie, the nature of the proposed cause of action and relief sought, and sufficient facts to enable the master to decide whether the case comes within one of the categories;

    (*b*) that the deponent believes the plaintiff has a good cause of action;

(c) the place or country where the defendant is, or probably may be found; and

(d) where the application is made under r 1(1)(c) (see Chapter 15), the grounds for the deponent's belief that there is between the plaintiff and the person on whom a writ has been served a real issue which the plaintiff may reasonably ask the Court to try.

The requirement in (c) is important since leave is normally given to serve the writ in a particular country, and service in any other country is bad (*Bounell* v *Preston* (1908) 24 TLR 756). If it is found that the defendant has moved elsewhere, an ex parte application should be made to the practice master on affidavit to amend the writ and previous order and issue a concurrent writ for service in the other country. Note that the fact that leave has been obtained does not preclude service in England.

In the Queen's Bench Division, application is made ex parte to a Queen's Bench Master. The affidavit should be left in the Masters' Secretary's Department (Room 122 at the Royal Courts of Justice). It may be collected there later with the Master's decision indorsed on it.

In the Chancery Division, the proposed writ and affidavit should be taken to the Masters' Appointments Clerk (Room 150, RCJ). The master either gives leave himself, where the issue is clear, or takes it to a judge, who will indorse the grant of leave on the writ. The writ is later returned to the solicitor to be issued at the Central Office. In a district registry action, it is sent for issue to the District Registry.

The principles applied in the exercise of the court's discretion are considered in Chapter 14.

If leave is granted, the order must limit a time within which the defendant to be served must acknowledge service. The time limits applicable to each foreign country are contained in the Extra Jurisdiction Tables (set out in Appendix 1).

2 Effecting service of writ

The amendments to RSC Ord 10, r 1, and Ord 11, r 5, made by the 1979 statutory instruments, abolishing the general requirement for personal service of writs, do *not* apply to service abroad. However, by Ord 11, r 5(3), a writ which is to be served out of the jurisdiction need not be served personally provided it is served in accordance with the law of the foreign country; and need not be served by the plaintiff or his agent if it is served pursuant to Ord 11, r 6 or 7.

Therefore, service by post is acceptable provided the law of the country where the writ is to be served permits. Where it is proposed to use this method, the Masters' Secretary's Department should always be consulted first.

Rule 5(2), provides that nothing in r 5 shall authorise any action in a foreign country which is contrary to that country's law.

Provision is made by Ord 11, r 6, for the service of writs abroad through foreign governments, judicial authorities and British Consuls. However, in the following countries service must be effected by the plaintiff or his agent direct (unless the country is a part to the Hague Convention: see below)

    (*a*)   Scotland, Northern Ireland, Eire, the Isle of Man, the Channel Islands;

    (*b*)   any independent Commonwealth country (for a list, inquire of Queen's Bench Masters' Secretary); and

    (*c*)   any colony or any associated state.

In the case of all other countries the methods of service depend upon to which (if any) conventions the country in question is a party.

(a) Convention countries

Austria, Belgium, Czechoslavakia, Denmark, Finland, France, Federal Republic of Germany, Greece, Hungary, Iraq, Israel, Italy, Laos, Lebanon, the Netherlands, Norway, Poland, Portugal, Spain, Sweden, Syria, Turkey and Yugoslavia are parties to, or accept, a civil procedure convention other than the Hague Convention (Ord 11, r 6(2)). Service may be effected either through the judicial authorities of the country where service is to be made or through a British consular authority in that country, subject to any provisions of the convention as to the nationality of persons who may be served. (Thus, in Denmark, Germany and Hungary, subjects of the country of service may not be served in this way; in Portugal, Portugese nations may only be so served in this manner.)

Although the editors of the *Supreme Court Practice* state (para 11/6/2) that, generally, service through British consular authorities of the country is preferable, it is possible to specify that either method should be used, ie whichever is the more convenient (r 6(7)). It should be noted that the Supreme Court Practice has changed its previous views as to the preferable mode of service.

The two methods of service mentioned are permissive, rather than exclusive. Thus service through an agent appointed by the plaintiff is a further alternative, where this is permitted by the local law. If an order for substituted service by post is made, and postal service is not allowed by the Convention with the particular country involved (eg France, Iraq and Italy), a judgment obtained following service by post will not be recognised in those countries.

Barbados, Belgium, Botswana, Denmark, Finland, France, Gibraltar, Israel, Japan, Luxembourg, Norway, Portugal, Malawi, Sweden, the Netherlands, Turkey, the United States of America and West Germany are parties to the Hague Convention (r 6(2A)). Service may be effected *either* through the authority designated under the Hague Convention in respect of that country: the Convention provides that each contracting state shall designate a central authority to receive requests for service from other contracting states and execute them (information about restrictions imposed by individual countries is available from Room 120); *or*, if the law of that country permits, through the judicial authorities of that country or a British consular authority in that country.

(b) Non-convention countries

The two methods of service available in respect of non-convention countries are through the country's government, where it is willing to effect service; or through a British consular authority in that country, except where such service is contrary to local law.

Service in the latter case is permitted in the following countries: Andorra, Argentine, Brazil (on British subjects only), Burma (not on local nationals), Chile, Colombia, Costa Rica, Cuba, the Dominican Republic, Ecuador, Ethiopia, Guatemala, Haiti, Honduras (on British subjects only), Iceland, Indonesia, Mexico, Monaco (on British subjects only), Morocco, Nicaragua, Panama, Paraguay, Peru, Salvador, South Africa, Tunisia (on British subjects only), Uruguay, and Vietnam (not on local nationals).

Argentina, Ecuador, Guatemala, and Panama do not accept the validity of a judgment based on such service. There are no facilities for service of foreign process in the Sheikdom of Muscat and Oman.

Service through the country's government is desirable in cases where there is any doubt whether service through a British consular agency would be contrary to local law.

An alternative method of service is throught the plaintiff's agent (see Ord 11, r 5) and there is no objection to this in Argentina (judgment based on such service may not be enforceable there), Chile, Cuba, Ethiopia, Japan, Mexico, Nicaragua, Sudan, the United States of America and Uruguay.

(c) Procedure

The plaintiff's solicitor should go personally to the Masters' Secretary's Department, Room 120, RCJ to lodge the following documents (which should not simply be posted):

(1) A request for service of the writ by one of the methods mentioned above. For a form of Request for Service see Appendix 2, Form 25. Note that by RSC Ord 11, r 8, the request must contain an undertaking by the person making it to be responsible personally for all expenses incurred by the Secretary of State in respect of the service requested and, on receiving due notification of the amount of those expenses, to pay that amount to the Finance Officer of the Office of the Secretary of State and to produce a receipt for the payment to the proper officer of the High Court;

(2) A copy of the writ and an additional copy for each person to be served. The writ is lodged in duplicate and sealed with the seal of the Supreme Court;

(3) A certified translation of the writ in the official language (or the appropriate local official language where there is more than one) of the country where service is to take place. The certificate of translation must contain the translator's full name, address and qualifications. This does not apply where the official language (or one of them) is English, or where the writ is to be served on a British subject by a British consular authority, unless a particular civil procedure convention even then requires a translation.

The documents lodged are sent by the Senior Master to the Parliamentary Under-Secretary of State to the Foreign Office with a request that he arranges for the writ to be served by the method indicated in head (1) above. As already mentioned, alternative methods may be requested, in which case the most convenient method is chosen (RSC Ord 11, r 6(7)).

One of the copy writs is served in the appropriate way and the other is later returned to Room 120, via the Foreign Office, with the official certificate of service (under RSC Ord 11, r 5) or note of inability to effect service. The certificate under r 5 is issued by the authority through which service was effected in the foreign country and, by r 5(7), a document purporting to be such a certificate is deemed to be genuine unless the contrary is proved. The Masters' Secretary's Department *then* send the copy writ to the following destinations:

in Probate and Divorce matters, to the Principal Probate Registry, Somerset House;

in Admiralty matters, to the Admiralty Registry;

in Queen's Bench and Chancery matters, to the Filing Department, RCJ;

in District Registry actions, to the appropriate District Registry.

They then inform the plaintiff's solicitor of the receipt of the certificate and the expense incurred, which fee is payable to the Finance Officer of the Diplomatic Service. A filing fee is payable if the certificate is sent for filing to the Filing Department.

If the plaintiff wishes to enter judgment because there has been no acknowledgement of service, he must produce the certificate of service. If it is in a foreign language, the plaintiff's solicitor should go to the Filing Department with a translator to translate the certificate and verify the same by affidavit. Only then will the court accept the translation.

In cases where the authorities are not involved and service is effected by the plaintiff's agent, the procedures in r 6 do not apply and the plaintiff must make his own arrangements. An affidavit of service must be sworn before a qualified person, details of which are contained in RSC Ord 41, r 12.

The Masters'Secretary's Department at Room 120 deals with service out of jurisdiction in all the High Court Divisions, including District Registry actions, and further information on the procedure may be obtained from there.

3 Service of other originating process

Apart from arbitration cases, for which there are special rules discussed below, the rules for service of a writ out of the jurisdiction apply to the service of an originating summons, notice of motion, or petition (r 9(1)).

Further, service out of the jurisdiction of any summons, notice or order issued, given or made in any proceedings is permissible with leave, but leave is not required for such service in any proceedings in which the writ or other originating process may be served without leave (r 9(4)). The appropriate procedure for applying for leave to serve an originating summons is the same as for a writ under RSC Ord 11, r 4(1)–(3). In relevant cases a time limit must be specified within which service must be acknowledged (r 9(6)).

The rules for service contained in RSC Ord 11, rr 5, 6 and 8, apply in relation to any document for the service of which out of the jurisdiction leave has been granted under r 9 (r 9(7)).

In arbitration cases, Ord 73, r 7(1), provides that service out of the jurisdiction of documents is permissible with the leave of the court provided that the arbitration to which the documents relate is governed by English law or has been, is being, or is to be held, within the jurisdiction.

(*a*) an originating summons for the appointment of an arbitrator or umpire;

(*b*) a notice of an originating motion to remove an arbitrator or umpire or to remit or set aside an award;

(*c*) an originating summons or notice of an originating motion under the Arbitration Act 1979; and

(*d*) any order made on such a summons or motion.

Service out of the jurisdiction of an originating summons for leave to enforce an award is permissible with the leave of the court whether or not the arbitration is governed by English law (r 7(1A)).

An application for the grant of leave under r 7 must be supported by an affidavit stating the grounds on which the application is made and showing in what place or country the person to be served is, or probably may be found; and no such leave will be granted unless it is made sufficiently to appear to the court that the case is a proper one for service out of the jurisdiction under r 7 (r 7(2)).

Order 11, rr 5, 6–8, apply in relation to any such summons, notice or order as is referred to above as they apply in relation to notice of a writ.

Basically, therefore, r 7 provides for an additional case for service out of the jurisdiction to those contained in Ord 11, r 1, and the practice here is the same as under Ord 11.

4 Amendments and appeals

Generally the rules as to amendments of the writ and statement of claim, with or without leave, apply in regard to writs for service out of the jurisdiction as in other actions. However, it is not permissible to add in the writ or statement of claim a cause of action other than that for which leave was given to issue and serve, *unless* the added cause of action is one in respect of which there is power to allow service out of the jurisdiction (*Waterhouse* v *Reid* [1938] 1 KB 743).

The new provisions of RSC Ord 12, dealing with acknowledgement of service and disputes as to the jurisdiction, are dealt with in Chapter 8. Reference should be made to that Chapter and in particular to an application under RSC Ord 12, r 8(1)(*c*), discussed there, which provides for an application by the defendant to discharge an order giving leave to serve a writ or notice on him out of the jurisdiction.

If the master refuses to give leave to issue and serve the writ, the plaintiff may appeal ex parte to the judge in chambers under RSC Ord 58, r 1, and from him, with leave to the Court of Appeal (under RSC Ord 58, r 7, Ord 59, r 14, and the Supreme Court Act 1981, s 18. If the master sets aside or refuses to set aside the order of service, the plaintiff or defendant may appeal to the judge in chambers and then with leave to the Court of Appeal under the provisions just noted.

5 Service on foreign states

The State Immunity Act 1978, s 12(6) (see Chapter 5, head 10), applies in the case of service on foreign states, so that a state may agree to the service of process in any manner it wishes, rather than under the rules (RSC Ord 11, r 7(4)).

Subject to r 7(4), where a person to whom leave has been granted under Ord 11, r 1, to serve a writ on a state (as defined in the 1978 Act, s 14) wishes to have the writ served on that state, he must lodge in the Central Office (Masters' Secretary's Department):

(*a*) a request for service to be arranged by the Secretary of State; and

(*b*) a copy of the writ; and

(*c*) except where the official language of the state is, or the official languages of that state include, english, a translation of the writ in the official language or one of the official languages of the state (r 7(1)).

A translation under (*c*) must be certified by the person making it to be a correct translation; and the certificate must contain a statement of that person's full name, address and qualifications for making the translation (r 7(2) and Ord 11, r 6(6)).

The documents lodged are sent by the Senior Master to the Secretary of State with a request that he arrange for the writ to be served on the state or the government in question, as the case may be (r 7(3)).

RSC Ord 11, r 8 (see head 2 above), applies to r 7. See also *Supreme Court Practice*, para 11/1/9.

Chapter 17

County Court Process

The procedure for serving county court process abroad is similar to that in the High Court, but it is not identical and accordingly the rules are set out in full in this chapter. They are contained in CCR Ord 8, which forms a complete code.

By CCR Ord 42, r 7(1), Ord 8 or any other provision of the rules relating to service out of the jurisdiction apply in relation to civil proceedings by the Crown, but do not apply in relation to proceedings *against* the Crown.

1 Application for leave

An application for leave to serve a process out of the jurisdiction is made to a registrar in the first instance (Ord 13, r 1(6)) and must be supported by an affidavit (or other evidence) stating the required matters (Ord 8, r 6(1)). A process is defined by Ord 8, r 1, as being an originating process (which includes a third-party notice), or an interlocutory process (which means a summons, order or notice issued, made or given in proceedings already commenced in or transferred to a county court).

Order 8, r 4 provides that service of an interlocutory process out of England and Wales is permissible with leave of the court on a person who is already a party to the proceedings and, in the case of a defendant, respondent or third party, has been served with the originating process but leave shall not be required for such service in any proceedings in which the originating process may by the CCR or under any Act be served out of England and Wales without leave.

The application must be made in accordance with the general procedure contained in Ord 13, r 1.

The affidavit must state the following (Ord 8, r 6(1)):

(*a*) in the case of a fixed date summons: that in the belief of the deponent, the applicant has a good cause of action; and

(*b*) in the case of any process: in what country and place the respondent is, or may probably be found, whether the respondent is a United Kingdom national or not and the grounds on which the application is made.

Further, where the application is made under r 2(1)(c) (see Chapter 15), the affidavit must show the grounds for the deponent's belief that there is between the applicant and the person on whom an originating process has been served a real issue which the applicant may reasonably ask the court to try.

By Ord 8, r 6(2) the judge may not grant leave unless it appears to him that the case is a proper one for service out of England and Wales.

Where an application is made for leave to serve a process in Scotland or Northern Ireland, an additional hurdle has to be cleared. By Ord 8, r 5(1), where it appears to the court that there may be a concurrent remedy in Scotland or Northern Ireland (as the case may be), the court must have regard to the comparative cost and convenience of proceedings in the district, or in the place of residence of the respondent, and particularly to the powers and jurisdiction of the sheriff courts in Scotland and of the county courts in Northern Ireland.

The court must have regard to the distance of the country of service in fixing the return day or, in the case of a default summons, fixing the time for delivering an admission or defence, or paying the total amount of the claim and costs into court (Ord 8, r 7). The return day should always be at least two months ahead though, by Ord 13, r 4, the time fixed may be extended. The Extra Jurisdiction Table (Appendix 1) may be referred to.

2 Methods of service

By Ord 8, r 8(1), where leave has been granted, service may, subject to the provisions of r 8, be effected through the court or by the applicant or his agent.

The method of service depends on the status of the country in which service is to be effected.

By Ord 8, r 8(2), where the country of service is a convention country, service may be effected through the court, or, if the convention permits, by the applicant or his agent. The term 'convention country' is defined by Ord 8, r 1, as meaning a foreign country with which a convention has been made relating to civil procedure including the service of documents issued from England or Wales in the foreign country and includes a country which is a part to the Hague Convention. For lists of these countries, see Chapter 16.

By Ord 8, r 8(4), where the country of service is not a convention country but is a country mentioned in r 8(5), service may be effected by the applicant or his agent, if and so far as the laws of the country of service permit. Order 8, r 8(5), lists the following countries:

(a) Scotland, Northern Ireland, the Isle of Man and the Channel Islands;

(b) any independent Commonwealth country outside the United Kingdom, and any territory administered by the government of such a country;

(c) any associated state;

(d) any colony;

(e) the Republic of Ireland.

By Ord 8, r 8(3), where the country of service is neither a convention country not a country mentioned in r 8(5), service may be effected through the court.

Order 8, r 8(6) provides that, where the respondent is a state, as defined in the State Immunity Act 1978, s 14 service must be effected through the court, except where the state has agreed to some other method of service.

3 Effecting service

Order 8, r 10 applies, with necessary modifications, where, in pursuance of an order for substituted service, a document is required to be transmitted through the court to the country of service (Ord 8, r 10(9)).

By Ord 8, r 10(1) and (2), where service is to be effected through the court, the applicant must file a request in that behalf (see Appendix 2, Form 24) together with a copy thereof, and two copies of the process to be served. The request must indicate whether the applicant wishes service to be effected:

(a) through the authority designated under the Hague Convention (see Chapter 15);

(b) through the foreign judicial authority;

(c) through a British consular authority;

(*d*) through the foreign government, where it is willing for service to be effected.

Where the party to be served is a state, as defined in the State Immunity Act 1978, s 14, the request must indicate this fact and that the applicant is willing for service to be effected by whatever method the Secretary of State may choose (Ord 8, r 10(3)).

Further, by Ord 8, r 10(4), the applicant must file with the request two copies of a translation of the process in the language of the country of service, certified by or on behalf of the applicant to be a correct translation. However, this does not apply where the official language or one of the official languages of the country of service is English. Neither does it apply where service is to be effected on a United Kingdom national directly through the British Consul, unless the country of service is a convention country and the convention requires a translation.

By Ord 8, r 10(5), the proper officer will seal the two copies of the process and the translations (if any), and forward them and the request to the Senior Master of the Supreme Court (Queen's Bench Division). RSC Ord 11, r 6(7) (see Chapter 16, head 2), applies to county court documents and the Senior Master sends any certificate or declaration of service received to the county court registrar (RSC ORd 11, r 10).

Order 8, r 10(6), provides that an official certificate or declaration upon oath or otherwise of the judicial authority, central authority or government of the country of service or of the British consular authority in that country, transmitted by the senior master to the county court registrar, will be received as evidence of the facts certified or declared with regard to the service or attempted service of the process.

Service is deemed to be good (by Ord 8, r 10(7)) where the process has been served: in accordance with the law of the country of service or in the manner in which default summonses are required to be served.

By Ord 8, r 10(8), where it appears from the certificate or declaration that the process has been duly served upon the respondent, the certificate or declaration shall be an equivalent substitute for any affidavit or certificate of service which would normally be required by the rules. If the respondent does not appear on the return day, the applicant must, before proceeding, file the official certificate or declaration, showing that the process has been duly served (Ord 8, r 10).

By Ord 8, r 9, the process, if served by the applicant or his agent, shall be served on the respondent by delivering it to him personally, and the normal rules as to personal service apply.

If the respondent does not appear on the return day, the applicant shall, before proceeding, file an affidavit showing that the process has been duly served (Ord 8, r 11).

4 Setting aside service

By Ord 8, r 12, the respondent may apply, on notice, to the court (ie initially to the registrar) to set aside the service of the process, or to discharge the order giving leave to serve the process out of the jurisdiction. Such an application is made under Ord 13, r 1.

The aggrieved respondent is not obliged to apply under Ord 8, r 12; the rule uses the word 'may'. He has the alternative remedy of applying to the High Court for an order of prohibition under the County Courts Act 1959, s 116 (see *Channel Coaling Company* v *Ross* [1907] 1 KB 145).

5 Matrimonial proceedings

Rule 117(1) of the MCR provides that any document in matrimonial proceedings may be served out of England and Wales *without leave* either in the manner prescribed by the MCR; or, where the proceedings are pending in the High Court, in accordance with RSC Ord 11, rr 5, 6; or, where the proceedings are pending in a divorce county court, in accordance with CCR Ord 8, rr 8–10.

The term 'matrimonial proceedings' is defined by the MCR, r 2(2), in a most convoluted manner, as any proceedings with respect to which rules may be made under the Matrimonial Causes Act 1973, s 50. It includes divorce proceedings, and proceedings under the Matrimonial Homes Act 1967, ss 1 and 7, and under the Married Women's Property Act 1882, s 17. It is recommended that reference is made to s 50 where there may be some doubt.

The expression 'in the manner prescribed by these Rules' includes personal service, service by ordinary or registered post, and service on a party's solicitor where one is acting for him (MCR, rr 118, 119).

Where the document is served in accordance with RSC Ord 11, the official certificate of service referred to in Ord 11, r 5(5), must, if the document was served personally, show the server's means of knowledge of the identity of the person served in addition to the other information required (MCR, r 117(2)).

By r 117(3), where the document is served in accordance with CCR Ord 8, rr 8–10, those rules are modified in the following manner:

(a) the document need not be served personally provided it is served in accordance with the law of the country of service;

(b) where the document is served personally, the official certificate or declaration of service under r 10(6) must show the server's means of knowledge of the identity of the person served; and

(c) where the method of service is through the court, r 10(7) is amended by deleting the alternative 'or in the manner in which default summonses are required to be served.'

Where the document to be served is a petition, the time limited for giving notice of intention to defend under the MCR, r 15, is based on the Extra Jurisdiction Tables set out in Appendix 1. However, since those tables are based on the period of fourteen days as the time for acknowledging service of a writ, and the time for giving notice of intention to defend a petition is eight days, each figure must be reduced by six days. The resulting figure is inserted in the appropriate place in the notice of proceedings (Form 5 in MCR Appendix 1).

Where the document is one specifying the date of hearing of any proceedings, the date is fixed using the same tables, making any necessary adjustments (MCR, r 117(5)).

MCR, r 117(4)(b), provides that if a petition is to be served other than in accordance with RSC Ord 11 or CCR Ord 8, rr 8–10; and there is reasonable ground for believing that the person to be served does not understand English; and the official language of the country of service (or one of the official languages) is not English, then the petition must be accompanied by a translation, approved by the registrar, of the notice in Form 5, in the official language of the country of service or, if there is more than one official language, in any one of those languages, appropriate to the place where service is to be effected.

Appendix 1

Extra Jurisdiction Tables

Table of times for entering appearance after service out of the jurisdiction of a notice of writ of summons or an originating summons to which an appearance is required to be entered and for serving of summonses, and for the return day of summonses, served out of the jurisdiction for hearing in the Queen's Bench Division.

Method of calculation The following table shows the number of days to be allowed for acknowledging service of a writ of summons or originating summons to which an acknowledgement of service is required.

(1) In the case of countries which are a party to the European Community Convention on Civil Jurisdiction and the Enforcement of Judgments, the period has been fixed at 21 days by the Civil Jurisdiction and Judgments Act 1982 and with regard to the dependant territories of those states it has been fixed for a period of 31 days.

(2) In respect of all other countries, the time allowed is calculated on the basis of allowing the time of air mail from the country plus the number of days between posts (with a minimum of three days) plus three days for delivery within the country, plus the normal 14 days for acknowledgement of service.

The ordinary form of order allowing service in any city or place abroad contains the additional words 'or elsewhere in the kingdom, [or republic or as may be] of   .'

Service of summonses Where a four-day summons is to be served abroad the period allowed for the service is seven days less than the time given below, and the period allowed between service and the date for hearing the summons is ten days less than the time given below. This method of calculation should be adapted for summonses requiring a longer or shorter period of notice.

Place or Country	Time for Acknow- ledgement of Service	Place or Country	Time for Acknow- ledgment of Service
	Days		Days
Abu Dhabi	22	Chad	25
Afghanistan	23	Chile	22
Albania	25	China	24
Algeria	22	Christmas Island	27
Angola	22	Cocos (Keeling) Islands	41
Anguilla	31	Colombia	22
Antigua	23	Comoros	23
Antilles (Netherlands)	31	Congo	25
Argentina	22	(People's Republic)	
Ascension	31	Corsica	21
Australia	25	Costa Rica	23
Austria	21	Cuba	24
Azores	23	Cyprus	31
Bahamas	22	Cyrenaica (see Libya)	21
Bahrain	22	Czechoslovakia	21
Balearic Islands	21	Denmark	21
Bangladesh	23	Djibouti	22
Barbados	23	Dominica	23
Belgium	21	Dominican Republic	23
Belize	23	Dubai	22
Benin	25	Ecuador	22
Bermuda	31	Egypt (Arab Republic)	22
Bhutan	28	El Salvador	
Bolivia	23	(Republic of)	25
Botswana	23	Equatorial Guinea	23
Brazil	22	Ethiopia	22
Brunei	25	Falkland Islands and	
Bulgaria	23	Dependencies	31
Burma	23	Faroe Islands	31
Burundi	22	Fiji	23
Cameroon	22	Finland	24
Canada	22	France	21
Canary Islands	22	French Guiana	31
Cape Verde Islands	25	French Polynesia	31
Caroline Islands	31	French West Indies	31
Cayman Islands	31	Gabon	25
Central African Republic	25	Gambia	22

Place or Country	Time for Acknow- ledgement of Service	Place or Country	Time for Acknow- ledgment of Service
	Days		*Days*
Germany Democratic		Laos	30
Republic of	21	Lebanon	22
Germany Federal		Lesotho	23
Republic of	21	Liberia	22
Ghana	22	Libya	21
Gibraltar	31	Liechtenstein	21
Greece	21	Luxembourg	21
Greenland	31	Macau	31
Grenada	24	Madeira	31
Guatemala	24	Madagascar	23
Guernsey	31	Malawi	23
Guyana	22	Malaya	24
Haiti	23	Maldive Islands	26
Holland (Netherlands)	21	Mali	25
Honduras	24	Malta	21
Hong Kong	31	Mariana Islands	26
Hungary	22	Marshall Islands	32
Iceland	22	Mauritania	23
India	23	Mauritius	22
Indonesia	22	Mexico	23
Iran	22	Monaco	21
Iraq	22	Montserrat	31
Ireland (Eire)	21	Morocco	22
Ireland (Northern)	21	Mozambique	23
Isle of Man	31	Nauru Island	36
Israel	22	Nepal	23
Italy	21	Netherlands	21
Ivory Coast	22	Nevis	24
Jamaica	22	New Caledonia	31
Japan	23	New Hebrides	
Jersey	31	(now Vanuatu)	29
Jordan	23	New Zealand	26
Kampuchea	38	New Zealand Island	
Korea, North	28	Territories	50
Kenya	22	Nicaragua	24
Korea, South	24	Niger, Republic of	25
Kuwait	22	Nigeria	22

Place or Country	Time for Acknow- ledgement of Service	Place or Country	Time for Acknow- ledgment of Service
	Days		Days
Norfolk Island	31	Solomon Islands	29
Norway	21	Somali Democratic	
Oman, Sultanate of	22	Republic	22
Pakistan	23	South Africa, Republic	
Panama, Republic of	26	of	22
Papua New Guinea	26	South Georgia (Falkland	31
Paraguay	22	Island Dependencies)	
Peru	22	South Orkneys	21
Philippines	23	South Shetlands	21
Pitcairn Island	31	Spain	21
Poland	21	Spanish Territories of	
Portugal	21	North Africa	31
Portuguese Timor	31	Sri Lanka	23
Puerto Rico	23	Sudan	22
Qatar	23	Suriname	22
Reunion	31	Swaziland	22
Rumania	22	Sweden	21
Russia (U.S.S.R.)	21	Switzerland	21
Rwanda	23	Syria	23
Sabah	23	Taiwan	23
St Helena	31	Tanzania	22
St Kitts-Nevis	24	Thailand	23
St Lucia	24	Tibet	34
St Pierre and Miquelon	31	Tobago	23
St Vincent Grenadians	24	Togo	22
Samoa (USA Territory)	30	Tonga	30
(See also Western Samoa)		Tortola	31
Sarawak	28	Trinidad & Tobago	23
Saudi Arabia	24	Tristan Da Cunha	31
Scotland	21	Tunisia	22
Senegal	22	Turkey	21
Seychelles	22	Turks & Caicos Islands	31
Sharjah	24	Uganda	22
Sierra Leone	22	Union of Soviet	
Singapore	22	Socialist Republics	21
Society Islands (French		United States of	
Polynesia)	31	America	22

Place or Country	Time for Acknow- ledgement of Service	Place or Country	Time for Acknow- ledgment of Service
	Days		Days
Upper Volta	23	Wake Island	25
Uruguay	22	Western Samoa	34
Vanuatu	29	Yemen Arab Republic	30
Vatican City State	21	Yemen (People's	22
Venezuela	22	Democratic Republic)	
Vietnam	28	Yugoslavia	21
Virgin Islands, British		Zaire	25
(Tortola)	31	Zambia	23
Virgin Islands USA	24	Zimbabwe	22

Appendix 2

Forms

Forms 1–13 and 15 are Queen's Bench Masters' Practice Forms. Forms 1–15 are published by the Solicitors' Law Stationery Society PLC and are reproduced here by permission.

Forms 16 and 17 are prescribed by the County Court (Forms) Rules 1982.

Forms 18–21 and 24 have been approved by the Lord Chancellor but are not prescribed by rule.

Forms 22 and 23 are court forms. Form 23 is published by Her Majesty's Stationery Office and is reproduced here by permission of the Controller.

1 Affidavit of service of writ (personal)

Affidavit of Service
of Writ *(Personal)*
(O. 13, r.7
O. 10, r.1(6))

IN THE HIGH COURT OF JUSTICE   19 .— .—No.

Division

Between

Plaintiff

AND

Defendant

(1) Name, address
and description of
the Deponent.

I, (¹)

of

MAKE OATH AND SAY AS FOLLOWS:—

1.   **I did** on   day the   day of   , 19 ,

(2) State where.

at (²)

personally serve

(3) "Each", *if more
than one,* or "one of
the above-named
Defendants".

(³)

the above-named Defendant

with a true copy of the Writ of Summons in this action.

2.   **The said copy Writ** was duly sealed with the seal of the Court office out of which it was issued and was accompanied by a prescribed form of Acknowledgment of Service.

(⁴)

Sworn at

the   day of   19

Before me,

A Commissioner for Oaths/Solicitor.

This affidavit is filed on behalf of the Plaintiff

PF122 (B36)

2 Affidavit of service of writ on individual by post

Affidavit of Service of Writ on Individual by Post (O. 10, r. 1(3) (a), 1 (6)).

IN THE HIGH COURT OF JUSTICE 19 .— .—No.
Division

Between

Plaintiff

AND

Defendant

(1) State name address and description of deponent.

I, (¹)

make oath and say as follows:

(2) Give name.

1. **That I did** serve the above-named defendant (²) with a true copy of the Writ of Summons in this action by posting the same on day, the day of 19 , by ordinary post First Class Mail in an envelope duly pre-paid and properly addressed to the said defendant at (³)

(3) State address in full.

2. **The said copy Writ** was duly sealed with the seal of the Court office out of which it was issued and was accompanied by a prescribed form of Acknowledgment of Service.

3. **The said letter** or envelope has not been returned by the Post Office through the Dead Letter Service.

(4) In the case of posting by the Plaintiff's Solicitor or any employee in his firm.
(5) Delete whichever is inapplicable.

4. **[That in my opinion]** [(⁴) **In the opinion of the Plaintiff]** (⁵) the said Writ of Summons so posted to the defendant will have come to his knowledge within seven days after the said date of posting thereof.

SWORN at

this day of 19

Before me,

A Commissioner for Oaths/Solicitor

This affidavit is filed on behalf of the Plaintiff

PF122A (B37)

3 Affidavit of service of writ on individual by insertion through letter-box

Affidavit of Service
of Writ on Individual
by Insertion through
Letter-box
(O 10, r. 1(3) (b),
1 (6)).
IN THE HIGH COURT OF JUSTICE

Division

19   .—   .—No.

Between

Plaintiff

AND

Defendant

(1) State name,
address and
description of
deponent.
I, (¹)

(2) Give name.
make oath and say as follows:

1. **That I did** serve the above-named defendant (²)

with a true copy of the Writ of Summons in this action by inserting the same through the Letter-Box for the address of the said defendant on   day, the   day of   ,19   , enclosed in a sealed envelope duly and properly addressed to the said defendant at (³)

(3) State address
in full.

2. **The said copy Writ** was duly sealed with the seal of the Court office out of which it was issued and was accompanied by a prescribed form of Acknowledgment of Service.

(4) In the case of
such insertion by the
Plaintiff's Solicitor or
any employee in
his firm.

(5) Delete
whichever is
inapplicable.

3. [**That in my opinion**] [(⁴) **In the opinion of the Plaintiff**] (⁵) the said Writ of Summons so inserted in the letter-box for the address of the defendant will have come to his knowledge within seven days after the said date of such insertion thereof.

SWORN at

this   day of   19

Before me,

A Commissioner for Oaths/Solicitor

This affidavit is filed on behalf of the Plaintiff

PF122B (B37C)

4 Affidavit of service of writ on partnership firm by post

Affidavit of Service
of Writ on
Partnership
Firm by Post
(O. 81, r. (2) (b)
O. 10, r. 1 (6))

IN THE HIGH COURT OF JUSTICE
                Division

                                              19   .—   .—No.

Between

                                                            Plaintiff

                                    AND

                                                            Defendant

(1) State name,
address and
description of
deponent.

I, (¹)

                make oath and say as follows :

(2) Name of firm.

                    1. **That I did** serve the above-named defendant firm (²)

                with a true copy of the Writ of Summons in this action by posting the same on
                          day, the   day of   19   , by ordinary post
                First Class Mail in an envelope duly pre-paid and properly addressed to the said

(3) State address
in full of principal
place of business of
defendant firm.

defendant firm at (³)

                    2. **The said copy Writ** was duly sealed with the seal of the Court office
                out of which it was issued and was accompanied by a prescribed form of
                Acknowledgment of Service.

                    3. **The said letter** or envelope has not been returned by the Post Office
                through the Dead Letter Service.

(4) In the case of
posting by the
Plaintiff's Solicitor or
any employee in his
firm.

(5) Delete
whichever is
inapplicable.

                    4. [**That in my opinion**] [(⁴) **In the opinion of the Plaintiff**] (⁵) the
                said Writ of Summons so posted to the above-named defendant firm will have come
                to the knowledge of one or more of the partners or a person having at the time of
                service the control or management of the partnership business there within seven
                days after the said date of posting thereof.

                SWORN at

                this   day of   19

                        Before me,

                    A Commissioner for Oaths/Solicitor

                        This affidavit is filed on behalf of the Plaintiff

PF122C (B37A)

5 Affidavit of service of writ on manager of partnership firm

Affidavit of Service on Manager of Partnership Firm (O. 81, r. 3, O. 10, r. 1 (6)).

IN THE HIGH COURT OF JUSTICE
Division

19 .— .—No.

Between

Plaintiff

AND

Defendant

(1) Name, address and occupation of the Deponent.

I, (¹)

of

make oath and say as follows:—

1. **I did** on day the day of 19 , at

(2) The insertion of the name is not essential.

being the principal place of business of the above-named Defendant Partnership within the jurisdiction of this Honourable Court, personally serve (²)

the person having at the time of such service the control or management of the said Partnership business there, with a true copy of the Writ of Summons in this action.

2. **The said copy Writ** was duly sealed with the seal of the Court office out of which it was issued and was accompanied by a prescribed form of Acknowledgment of Service.

3. **I did** at the time of the said service deliver to the person so served as aforesaid a notice in writing that the said Writ of Summons was served upon him as the person having the control or management of the Partnership business of the said Defendant firm.

SWORN at

this day of 19

Before me,

A Commissioner for Oaths/Solicitor

This affidavit is filed on behalf of the Plaintiff

6 Notice of service on Manager of partnership

Notice of Service
on Manager of
Partnership
(O. 81 r. 3)

IN THE HIGH COURT OF JUSTICE

Division

19 .— .—No.

Between

Plaintiffs

AND

Defendants

Take notice that the Writ served herewith is served on you as the person having the control or management of the partnership business of the above-named Defendant firm of

(1) If the person served with the Writ is served in the two capacities of Manager and Partner this clause should be *left standing*. If he is served as Manager only, it should be *struck out.* [(¹) and also as a partner in the said firm.]

Plaintiffs Solicitors.

PF173 (B36C)

7 Affidavit of service of writ on body corporate by post

Affidavit of Service
of Writ on Body
Corporate by Post.
(O. 65, r. 3 (2).
O. 10, r. 1 (6))

IN THE HIGH COURT OF JUSTICE
Division

19 .— .—No.

Between

Plaintiff

AND

Defendant

(1) State name, address and description of deponent.

I, (¹)

(2) Name of corporation.

make oath and say as follows:
1. **That I did** serve the above-named defendant corporation (²)

with a true copy of the Writ of Summons in this action by posting the same on day, the day of 19 , by ordinary post First Class Mail in an envelope duly pre-paid and properly addressed to the said defendant corporation at (³)

(3) State address in full of registered or principal office of defendant body corporate.

2. **The said copy Writ** was duly sealed with the seal of the Court office out of which it was issued and was accompanied by a prescribed form of Acknowledgment of Service.

3. **The said letter** or envelope has not been returned by the Post Office through the Dead Letter Service.

(4) In the case of posting by the Plaintiff's solicitor or any employee in his firm.
(5) Delete whichever is inapplicable.
(6) Mayor, or Chairman, or Town Clerk, or other similar officer of the above-named defendant corporation referred to in R.S.C. Ord. 65, r. 3 (1), as the case may be.

4. [That in my opinion] [(⁴) **In the opinion of the Plaintiff**] (⁵) the said Writ of Summons so posted to the above-named defendant corporation will have come to the knowledge of the (⁶) within seven days after the said date of posting thereof.

SWORN at

this day of 19

Before me,

A Commissioner for Oaths/Solicitor

This affidavit is filed on behalf of the Plaintiff

PF122D (B37B)

8 Affidavit of service of writ on body corporate by insertion through letter-box

Affidavit of Service
of Writ on Body
Corporate by
Insertion through
Letter-box
(O. 65, r. 3 (2),
O. 10, r. 1 (6))

IN THE HIGH COURT OF JUSTICE

Division

19   .—   .—No.

Between

Plaintiff

AND

Defendant

(1) State name, address and description of deponent.

I, (¹)

make oath and say as follows:

(2) Name of corporation.

1. **That I did** serve the above-named defendant corporation (²)

with a true copy of the Writ of Summons in this action by inserting the same through the Letter-Box for the address of the said defendant corporation on   day,

(3) State address in full of registered or principal office of defendant body corporate.

the   day of   19   , enclosed in a sealed envelope duly and properly addressed to the said defendant corporation at (³)

2. **The said copy Writ** was duly sealed with the seal of the Court office out of which it was issued and was accompanied by a prescribed form of Acknowledgment of Service.

(4) In the case of such insertion by the Plaintiff's solicitor or any employee in his firm.
(5) Delete whichever is inapplicable.
(6) Mayor, or Chairman, or Town Clerk, or other similar officer of the above-named defendant corporation referred to in R.S.C. Ord. 65, r. 3 (1), as the case may be.

3. **[That in my opinion]** [(⁴) **In the opinion of the Plaintiff]** (⁵) the said Writ of Summons so inserted in the Letter-Box for the address of the above named defendant corporation will have come to the knowledge of the (⁶)   within seven days after the said date of such insertion thereof.

SWORN at

this   day of   19

Before me,

A Commissioner for Oaths/Solicitor

This affidavit is filed on behalf of the Plaintiff

9 Affidavit of service of writ on English limited company

Affidavit of Service
on English Limited
Company
(Companies Act,
1948, s.437)
(O.10, r. 1(6)).

IN THE HIGH COURT OF JUSTICE

Division

Between   19 .— .—No.

Plaintiff

AND

Defendant

(1) Name, address
and description of
Deponent.

I, (¹)

of

make oath and say as follows:—

(2) If posted, date
of posting

1. I did on (²)   day, the   day of   19 .
serve the above-named Defendants with a true copy of the Writ of Summons
in this action, by (³)

(3) "leaving the
same at" (place of
service) or "sending
the same by (first)
(second) class mail on
the .... day
of .... 19...
in a prepaid letter or
envelope addressed
to the Company at"
(address)'

which is the registered office of the said Defendant Company.

2. The said copy Writ was duly sealed with the seal of the Court office out of
which it was issued and was accompanied by a prescribed form of Acknowledgment of Service.

Sworn at

the   day of   19

Before me,

A Commissioner for Oaths/Solicitor.

This affidavit is filed on behalf of the Plaintiff

PF126 (B36D)

10 Affidavit of service of originating summons (general form)

Affidavit of Service
of Originating
Summons
(General Form)
(O. 65 &
O. 7, r. 2(1))

IN THE HIGH COURT OF JUSTICE   **19** .— .—No.

Division

[**District Registry]**

Between

Plaintiff

AND

(1) Name, address
and occupation
of Deponent

I,(¹)

of

Defendant

make oath and say as follows :—

1. **I did on**   day the   day of   19   ,

(2) Place of
service

at(²)

(3) Insert name(s)

personally serve the Defendant   herein(³)

with a true copy of the Originating Summons in this action.

2. **The said copy** Originating Summons was duly sealed with the seal of the Court Office out of which it was issued and was accompanied by a prescribed form of Acknowledgment of Service.

Sworn at

the   day of   19

Before me,

A Commissioner for Oaths/Solicitor.

This affidavit is filed on behalf of the Plaintiff.

PF133 (B36E)

11 Affidavit of service of originating summons (expedited form)

Affidavit of Service
of Originating
Summons
(Expedited Form)
(O.65)

IN THE HIGH COURT OF JUSTICE   19 .— .—No.

Division

[**District Registry]**

Between

                                                              Plaintiff

                                    AND

                                                              Defendant

(1) Name, address.
and description of
Deponent.

I, (¹)

                              make oath and say as follows:—

1. **I did** on   , the   day of   19 ,

(2) Place of service.

at (²)

in the County of

(3) Name(s) of
persons served.

personally serve (³)

the [Defendant   ] herein [each] with a true copy of the Originating Summons
in this action.

2. **The said copy** Originating Summons was duly sealed with the seal of the
Court office out of which it was issued and was accompanied by a prescribed
form of Acknowledgment of Service.

3. **The copy** of the Originating Summons so served as aforesaid bore on the
face thereof due notice to the person served therewith of the place where he
was required to attend and the day and hour of such attendance, or if such date
and place has not been fixed at a date time and place to be fixed.

SWORN at

the   day of   19

Before me,

                    A Commissioner for Oaths/Solicitor.

This affidavit is filed on behalf of the Plaintiff.

12 Affidavit on application for substituted service

Affidavit on Application
for Substituted
Service (O. 65, r. 4 &
O. 10, r. 1(6)). **IN THE HIGH COURT OF JUSTICE**

                        Division   **19**   .—   .—No.

Between

                                              Plaintiff

                    and

                                            Defendant

(1) Name, address and occupation of deponent.   **I, (¹)**

make oath and say as follows:—

    1. **Having** been directed by

                                          to serve the

above-named Defendant

with a copy of the Writ of Summons in this action which has been duly sealed with the seal of the Court office out of which the Writ was issued accompanied by a prescribed form of Acknowledgment of Service,

(2) Describe efforts to effect service.   I did on   day the   day of   19
attend for the purpose of serving a copy of the said Writ at (²)

Form 12 contd

2. I did accordingly attend at the said place for the purpose aforesaid at
    o'clock in the   noon on   day the said
day of   19   and then saw   person
who represented   self to be and whom I believe to have been the
                               of the said Defendant, who informed me that

I again stated to the said person the nature of my business and told h   that
I would call again for the purpose of seeing the said Defendant and serving h
with a copy of the said Writ at the said place on the   day of
19   at   o'clock in the   noon and requested h   to inform
the said Defendant thereof which h   promised to do. I also on the said
day of   19   caused to be sent by prepaid post addressed to
the said Defendant at
a letter confirming the appointment and informing h   of the nature thereof and
enclosing a copy of the said Writ.

3. I did accordingly attend at the said place for the purpose aforesaid at
    o'clock in the   noon of   day the said   day of
                19   and then saw   person who
represented   self to be and whom I believe to have been the
                of the said Defendant, who informed me that

Form 12 contd

4. I did not on any of the said occasions see the said Defendant and I say that I have done all I possibly could do to serve the said Defendant with a true copy of the said Writ but I have not been able to do so, and for the reasons aforesaid I believe that the said Writ has come to the knowledge of the said Defendant and that he wilfully keeps out of the way to avoid personal service thereof.

5. I have made all reasonable efforts and used all due means in my power to serve the said copy Writ accompanied by an Acknowledgment of Service but I have not been able to do so.

(1) Specify method of substituted service asked for.

6. (1)

SWORN at

.

.

.

this   day of   19

Before me,

A Commissioner for Oaths/Solicitor.

This affidavit is filed on behalf of the Plaintiff.

PF120 (B35)

13 Affidavit of substituted service by post

Affidavit of
Substituted Service
by Post
(O. 65, r. 4
O. 10, r. 1(6)).

IN THE HIGH COURT OF JUSTICE
Division

Between 19 —. .—No.

Plaintiff

AND

Defendant

(1) Name, address
and occupation of
Deponent.

I, (¹)
of

make oath and say as follows—

1.   **That I did** serve the above-named Defendant
with a true copy of the Writ of Summons in this action
and a true copy of the order of   dated the
day of   19   , for substituted service herein, by posting
the same by   class mail at the Post Office at
on   the   day of   19   ,
in a prepaid letter or envelope, addressed to the said Defendant   at
pursuant to the
said order.

2.   **The said copy Writ** was duly sealed with the seal of the Court office
out of which it was issued and was accompanied by a prescribed form of
Acknowledgment of Service.

Sworn at

this   day of   19

Before me,

This affidavit is filed on behalf of the Plaintiff

PF129 (B36B)

14 Affidavit of service of summons or notice for further directions

Affidavit of Service
of Summons or
Notice for further
Directions

IN THE HIGH COURT OF JUSTICE 19 .— .—No.

Queen's Bench Division

Between

Plaintiff

AND

Defendant

(1) Name, address
and occupation of
Deponent.

I, (¹)

of

Solicitor   for the above-named

make oath and say as follows:—

I did on   day the   day of   19

(2) "4 o'clock" or
"12 noon," if served
on Saturday.

before [after] the hour of   (²) in the afternoon, serve

(3)   Or   "the
above-named
Plaintiff"   (or
"Defendant") who
appeared in person.
(4) "Summons"
or   "Notice   for
further directions"
as the case may be.
(5) If by post
continue "by post-
ing it at the post
office at
in a pre-paid
envelope addressed
to the said
at   "
(6) "His clerk,"
or "his servants."

Solicitor   for the above-named (³)

in this action, with a true copy of the (⁴)

now produced and shewn to me,

marked A, by (⁵) leaving it at

being the address for service in this action with (⁶)   there.

Sworn at

this   day of   19

Before me,

A Commissioner for Oaths.

(7) "Plaintiff" or
"Defendant."

This affidavit is filed on behalf of the (⁷)

(B24)

15 Affidavit of service of summons under Order 14

Affidavit of Service of Summons under Order 14 (O. 65, r. 5)

IN THE HIGH COURT OF JUSTICE   19   .—   .—No.

Queen's Bench Division

Between

Plaintiff

AND

Defendant

(1) Name, address and occupation of Deponent.

I,(¹)

of

Solicitor for the above-named Plaintiff

make oath and say as follows:—

(2) Insert "four in the afternoon" if served on weekdays, or "twelve noon" if served on Saturday.

1.   **I did** on   day the   day of   19

before [after] the hour of (²)   serve

(3) If Defendant appeared in person say, "the above-named Defendant, who appeared in person."

(³)

Solicitor for the above-named Defendant

in this action with a true copy of the Summons now produced and shown to me marked **A**, together with a true copy of the affidavit of

(4) If any exhibits add "and the exhibits therein referred to."

(⁴)

(5) If served by post "by posting them at the post office at in a prepaid envelope addressed to the said at."

(⁵) by leaving them at

being the address for service in this action.

Sworn at

the   day of   19

Before me,

A Commissioner for Oaths.

PF138 (B24A)

16 Certificate of service

Case No.

I certify that the summons of which this is a true copy was served by me on [date]

Service was effected

(a) By leaving it at [posting it to] the address stated on the summons [to be the registered office of the Company].

(b) At the address stated in the summons [or at   ]

by delivering it to the defendant personally [or to

apparently not less than 16 years old, who promised to give it to the defendant on the same day or on   ]

(c) By posting it the defendant on
at the address stated on the summons in accordance with the certificate of the plaintiff or his solicitor

(d) By posting it to the defendant on _____
pursuant to the
certificate at [1] below

(e) By inserting it, enclosed in an envelope addressed to the defendant, in the letter box at the address stated on the summons for the reasons at [1]

Bailiff/Officer of the Court

([1]) I have reason to believe the summons will reach the defendant in sufficient time, because:

Bailiff

Or I certify that this summons has not been served for the following reasons:

Bailiff/Officer of the Court

N12

17 Certificate of service (firm)

Case No.

I certify that the summons of which this is a true copy, was served by me on [date]

Service was effected

(a) by delivering it at the address stated in the summons or at

to

a partner in [or who stated that he was a partner in] the defendant firm [or who stated that he carried on business in the name of   ]:

(b) by delivering it at the address stated in the summons or at
to a person who did not give his name, but stated that he was a partner in the defendant firm [or that he carried on business in the name of   ]:

(c) by delivering it at the address stated in the summons or at
being the principal place of business of the defendant firm within the district of this Court to
the person [or (1) to a person] who had appeared to have the control or management of the business there.

(1) If the name is not known.

(d) by posting it to the defendant firm on
at the address stated in the summons, in accordance with the certificate of the plaintiff or his solicitor.

(e) by posting it to the defendant firm on
pursuant to the certificate at (2) below.

(f) by inserting it, enclosed in an envelope addressed to the defendant firm, in the letter box at the address stated in the summons for reasons at (2).

Bailiff/Officer of the Court

(2) I have reason to believe the summons will reach the defendant firm in sufficient time, because:

Bailiff

Or I certify that this summons has not been served for the following reasons:

Bailiff/Officer of the Court

18 Affidavit of service

| | **In the** | **County Court** |

BETWEEN ....*Plaintiff,*

AND..*Defendant.*

Case No.

I,   [*full names and occupation of deponent*]
[*address*]   make oath and say as
follows:—

1. That I am over 16 years of age and
   (a) acting as agent for the plaintiff,
   [*or* (b) employed by   of
   [solicitor, acting as agent for
   of
   solicitor for the above-named plaintiff.]

2. That I did on the   serve the summons, a copy of which is
   attached and marked "A", on [*insert name of person served*]
   (a) by delivering it to the said defendant personally, at [*State place of Service.*]

FIRM

   [*or* (b) by delivering it at
   to [*insert name of person served*]   who stated that he
   was a partner in the defendant firm [*or* who carried on] [*or* who stated that he
   carried on] business in the name of the defendant firm.
   [*or* (c) by delivering it at
   to a person who did not give his name but stated that he [was a partner in] [*or*
   carried on business in the name of] the defendant firm.
   [*or* (d) by delivering it at
   being the principal place of business of the defendant firm within the district of this
   Court to [*insert name of person served*]   the person who had or
   appeared to have the control or management of the business there].

REGISTERED COMPANY

   [*or* (e) by leaving it [*or* by sending it by 1st class post on the previous day [*or* by
   2nd class post on   ] in a
   prepaid envelope addressed to the Defendant Company] at the address stated in
   the summons to be the registered office of the Defendant Company.]

SUB SERVICE

   [*or* (f) by sending it on the previous day by registered post together with a sealed
   copy of the order for substituted service of the summons, addressed to the
   defendant at
   in accordance with the order.]

3. That at the same time I paid or offered to [*insert name of person served*]
   the sum of   for his/her expenses (and loss of time).

Sworn at   in the
   of   this   }
         day of   19
                     Before me

            Officer of a Court, appointed by the judge to take Affidavits
Indorse the copy summons thus:– This paper marked 'A' is the copy summons
referred to in the attached affidavit.

This affidavit is filed on behalf of the plaintiff.

19 Notice of service of default summons

```
┌─────────────────────────────────────────────────────────────┐
│                         -                                     │
│                                                               │
│                                                               │
│                                                               │
│                  In the              County Court             │
│                                                               │
│                                      Case No.                 │
│     To the Plaintiff                                          │
│       TAKE NOTICE that the defendant was served with the      │
│                                                               │
│     summons on                                                │
│                                                               │
│                                 Dated                         │
│                                                               │
│                                      _____ │
│                                                               │
│                                                               │
│                                                               │
└─────────────────────────────────────────────────────────────┘
```

N222

20 Notice of non-service (general)

```
┌─────────────────────────────────────────────────────────────┐
│                                                               │
│                                                               │
│                  In the              County Court             │
│                                                               │
│                                      Case No.                 │
│     To the Plaintiff                                          │
│        TAKE NOTICE that the summons/application/order in this │
│     action has not been served, for the following reason:    │
│                                                               │
│     [If you have reason to believe that the defendant is      │
│     still at the address stated in the request for the        │
│     summons, you may request bailiff service at that address  │
│     on payment of the appropriate fee]¹                       │
│        [The summons/application/order has been returned to    │
│     the Home Court]                                           │
│     ¹Delete as applicable                                     │
│                                                               │
│                                 Dated                         │
│                                                               │
│                                      _____ │
│                                                               │
│                                                               │
└─────────────────────────────────────────────────────────────┘
```

N216

21 Certificate for postal service

In the   **County Court**

BETWEEN ....*Plaintiff,*   **Case No.**
AND..*Defendant.*

I request that [*state surname and where known initials or forenames*]
be served with the summons/application/order/in this action by post. I certify that I
have reason to believe that the summons/application/order if sent to the defendant(s)
at the address stated in the request will come to his/their knowledge in time for
him/them to comply with the requirements of the document served.

   I/The plaintiff understand(s) that:—

   1. if judgment is obtained as a result of postal service and is afterwards set aside on
the grounds that the service did not give the defendant adequate notice of the
proceedings I (the plaintiff) may be ordered to pay the costs of setting aside the
judgment; OR

   2. no order of commitment will be made against the defendant served by post
unless he appears at the hearing of the judgment summons or the judge is satisfied
that the summons came to his knowledge in sufficient time for him to appear; OR

   3. the witness will not be fined for failing to appear at the hearing unless the judge
is satisfied that the summons came to his knowledge in sufficient time to enable him
to appear and that he received a sum of money to compensate him for loss of time
and his travelling expenses.

                              Dated
                              Signed Plaintiff (Solicitor)

N219

22 Request for bailiff to serve petition

In the   **County Court**
                                        In the Divorce Registry

BETWEEN ....*Petitioner,*   **No. of 19**
AND..*Respondent.*

   I hereby request that the   respondent be served by the court
bailiff with the   petition in this matter

   The full name of the   respondent is

   The address (in England and/or Wales) at which bailiff service should be attempted
is

   I enclose/do not have a recent photograph of the respondent.

     Signed

     (Solicitors for the) Petitioner

     Address

     Telephone

D89/379

23 Affidavit in support of application to dispense with service of petition on respondent

IN THE   COUNTY COURT[1]

(1) *Delete as appropriate*

No.

IN THE DIVORCE REGISTRY[1]

BETWEEN   Petitioner

and   Respondent

READ THE NOTES OF GUIDANCE CAREFULLY BEFORE ANSWERING THE QUESTIONS AND EXHIBIT TO YOUR AFFIDAVIT ALL CORRESPONDENCE RELATING TO THE RESPONDENT'S WHEREABOUTS. ALL QUESTIONS MUST BE ANSWERED

QUESTION	ANSWER
1. On what date and at what address did you and the respondent last live together? State the date and address.	
2. Where did the respondent live after the parting? State the address (or addresses) and the result of enquiries made at that address (or those addresses)	
3. When was the respondent last seen or heard of? State the date and circumstances, including brief details of all enquiries made to trace the respondent as a result of this information.	

D 13B

Form 23 contd

QUESTION	ANSWER
4. What relatives or friends of the respondent are known to you? State their names, addresses and relationship and the enquiries you have made of each of them and with what result.	
5. Was the respondent in employment at or after the date of the parting? State the name and address of the respondent's last known employer, the respondent's occupation and the result of your enquiry of that employer.	
6. (a) Had the respondent, to your knowledge, a bank or building society account? (b) Was the respondent a member of a trade union or professional organisation? State details of the results of any enquiries that you have made of these bodies.	

Form 23 contd

QUESTION	ANSWER
7. Is there a magistrates' court order for maintenance in force? State the result of any enquiry you have made of that court relating to the respondent's whereabouts.	
8. What other enquiries have you made, or information do you have concerning the whereabouts of the respondent? State brief details.	

I,   *(full name)*

of   *(full residential address)*

                                                  (occupation)

make oath and say as follows:—

1. I am the petitioner in this cause.

2. The answers to Questions 1—8 above are true.

3. I produce the documents referred to in paragraphs 2,3,4,5,6,7 and 8[1] and marked...

(1) Delete as appropriate

4. I know of no other enquiry that can be made which might lead to the respondent being traced.

5. I ask the Court to make an order dispensing with service of the petition on the respondent or such other order as the Registrar thinks fit.

SWORN at   )

in the County of   )

this   day of   19   )

        Before me,

(2) Delete as appropriate   A Commissioner for Oaths
Officer appointed by the Court[2]
to take Affidavits.

D13B

24 Request for service out of England and Wales through the court

	In the	County Court
		Case No.

1. Date of Order giving leave to serve
   out of England and Wales.

2. Nature of process to be served.

3. Name of Country in which service is
   to be effected.

4. Name of party to be served.

5. Is the party to be served a State as
   defined in S14 of the State Immunity
   Act 1978?   Yes ☐   No ☐

6. Address of party to be served.

7. Is party to be served a United Kingdom
   National?   Yes ☐   No ☐

Service is desired—
   [1] through the authority designated under the Hague Convention
   [1] through the judicial authority of
   [1] through a British consular authority at
   [1] through the Government of
[where the government is willing to effect service]
   [1] Delete as appropriate.

I/We request that the above-mentioned process may be served through the Court.
I/We personally undertake to be responsible for all expenses incurred by Her
Majesty's Principal Secretary of State for Foreign and Commonwealth Affairs or the
senior master in respect of the service requested, and on receiving notice of the
amount of such expenses to pay them.
*[1] I am/We are willing for service to be effected by whatever method the Secretary of
State may chose[2].
[2] Delete if the answer to question 5 above is No.

(Signed Plaintiff or other Party or his Solicitor.)

25 Request for service of document abroad

I hereby request that the writ of summons [*or as may be describing the document*] in this action be sent through the proper channel to [*name of country*] for service on the [*defendant*]   , at   , or elsewhere in [*name of country*] and that it may be served

    (i)   through the government of
          (*where the Government is willing to effect service*)
   (ii)   through the judicial authority of
  (iii)   through the authority designated under the Hague Convention
  (iv)   through a British Consular authority at

                  (*delete which methods not desired*).

I hereby undertake to be responsible personally for all expenses incurred by the Secretary of State in respect of the service requested and, on receiving due notification of the amount of those expenses, to pay that amount to the Finance Officer of the office of the Secretary of State and to produce a receipt for the payment to the proper officer of the High Court.

Dated the   day of   19 .

                            (*Signature of party or solicitor*).

Index

179